BOWIEODYSSEY72

Also by Simon Goddard

Bowie Odyssey 71
Bowie Odyssey 70
The Comeback
Rollaresque
Simply Thrilled
Ziggyology
Mozipedia
Songs That Saved Your Life

BOWIEODYSSEY72

SIMONGODDARD

OMNIBUS PRESS

London / New York / Paris / Sydney / Copenhagen / Berlin / Madrid / Tokyo

Note to the reader: The following narrative takes place in 1972 and contains language and prevailing attitudes of the time which some readers may find offensive. The publishers wish to reassure that all such instances are there specifically for reasons of historical social context in order to accurately describe the period concerned.

Copyright © 2022 Omnibus Press
(A division of the Wise Music Group
14–15 Berners Street, London, W1T 3LJ)

Cover designed by Fabrice Couillerot
Picture research by Simon Goddard

Paperback ISBN 978-1-913172-48-0
Hardback ISBN 978-1-913172-49-7

A catalogue record for this book is available from the British Library.

Typeset by Evolution Design & Digital Ltd (Kent)
Printed in Malta

www.omnibuspress.com

BOWIECONTENTS72

'We fail to see any comparison between Marc Bolan and that gay creep David Bowie. We do not think that Bowie will be referred to in later years, as we're sure Marc will be.' – *DEBBIE & LYNN, David Bowie Extermination Society*

'Why on earth do so many turn on to that freak-faced pop puff David Bowie – one look at him surely makes you want to vomit. There are so many fantastic artists around now – like Harry Nilsson, Slade, Rod Stewart – that it seems impossible anybody should want to listen to Bowie's crappy music.' – *AL DELDERFIELD, David Bowie Extermination Unit*

LETTERS TO *RECORD MIRROR*, SEPTEMBER 1972

ONE

'Hello, we're here to see David Bowie.'

THE RECEPTIONIST FLITS HER LASHES at the rakish duo who've just strode out of the lift and up to her desk. Shoulder-length hair, casual groovy clobber, smelling of Gauloises and Crosby, Stills & Nash. They might be musicians.

'We're from *Melody Maker*.'

She smiles, chin dipping the softest of nods. But of course.

The one with the moustache a bit like Jason King's is commonly 'Mick', though he'd much rather everyone call him 'Michael' like his print byline. He's been a staff writer on the world's biggest-selling music weekly for almost two years, ever grateful to have escaped the local Midlands newspaper where his own entertainment column offered weekly respite to 'the tinker problem' and calls to bring back the birch for skinhead vandals. Now, instead of interviewing former *Crossroads* actress Sue Nicholls about her Walsall roots he makes a living arguing about Goebbels with John Lennon.

Michael's tousled accomplice with the laughing eyes and coat-hanger grin refusing to share their joke is called Barrie. He clutches a brown doctor's bag plastered with a tatty mosaic of band tour-pass stickers. Nobody, including Jan the receptionist, would be surprised to learn it doesn't contain any stethoscope. Rather, the more shamanic medicinal tools of an umbrella, a flash and the Pentax Spotmatic which has captured

1

the souls of The Beatles, The Who, Jimi Hendrix, Led Zeppelin and every other *Melody Maker* frontpager marshalled before his lens by the drowsiest of voices with the softest of Durham twangs.

Together, Michael Watts's words and Barrie Wentzell's pictures help the *Maker* sell 174,000 copies a week – more than its popsier sister paper *Disc and Music Echo*, more than its deadliest rival the *New Musical Express*, more than the still too serious *Sounds* and the much too waggish *Record Mirror* – the reason why the *Maker* dares to call itself 'the Bible of rock', even if it's edited by a 34-year-old former chess champion who in his owlish spectacles, kipper tie and combover seems to have missed his true vocation as a BBC weatherman. Not that it matters to Ray Coleman. At the newsstands his paper continues to checkmate the competition. He places his grandmaster's trust in the instincts of his all-male staff who, when not kicking sellotaped copies of last week's issue around the office, or typing themselves sober after another boozy lunch in the Red Lion, gently persuade him to fill its pages according to their own individual tastes. Which is why, in spite of Ray's partial misgivings, Michael and Barrie are here in Regent Street this dour January morning.

'To see David Bowie.'

It's *Hunky Dory* that swung it. The album David brought out just before Christmas, when Michael received his copy accompanied by a press release instructing him to 'Dig it, with special ears'. And so he dug, and kept digging until concluding in this week's *Maker* review: *'It's not only the best album Bowie has ever done, it's also the most inventive piece of songwriting to have appeared on record for a considerable time.'* He was still swooning about it at yesterday's editorial meeting when he successfully pitched to follow his rapturous appraisal with an interview feature on *Hunky Dory*'s creator. One phone call to the record company is all it took to arrange this morning's appointment at the offices of David's management, Gem Music.

'Take a seat,' smiles Jan, picking up a phone as Michael and Barrie sink their bony backsides into the cushions of the reception sofa, eyes twitching from carpet to chrome to potted plant to coffee table spread with glossy magazines which neither pick up.

The last time anyone from the *Maker* interviewed David was last April when jocular features editor Chris Welch took him for a pint in the Red

Lion to find out why he wore a dress on the cover of his current LP. The headline ran: 'WHY DOES DAVID BOWIE LIKE DRESSING UP IN LADIES' CLOTHES?'

This is the singer who Michael still expects to meet today, one he's already described in print as *'a priest of high camp'*, his inquisitive nose chasing the fresh scent adding an increasingly florid note to rock's traditional sweaty bouquet. In the past two months Michael has sat before Marc Bolan as he brushed the curls from his eyes discussing his 'bisexual appearance' and watched Rod Stewart clamber out of a white Lamborghini reeking of blondes and Blue Nun only to explain 'the queer bit' in his stage presence. Meanwhile, his *Maker* colleagues and print rivals have been heard muttering above ashtray and beermat, chewing the names of possible new genres: 'queer rock', 'gay rock' and 'camp rock'. But as Rod told him only the other week, flicking a speck of dust from his scarlet velvet suit, 'Anything glamorous is a bit camp.' The effeminate pose is in season and Michael comes to Gem's offices today prepared to meet another gaudy blossom. So does Barrie, who lodges deep in the glorious Gomorrah of Soho where he's been known to play the occasional game of Scrabble with Quentin Crisp. The men from the *Maker* are nothing if not unshockable.

'If you just follow me, please.'

Jan escorts them down a corridor, past half-open doors teasing with muffled conversations, faint music and trilling phones. She stops, giving one a cursory knock, in the same instant opening it wide enough to poke her head round. They hear her say, 'David? *Melody Maker* are here.' Then, with a polite smile, she steps out of their way as the door swings open, allowing them a clear view inside . . .

SOMEWHERE, NOT SO FAR AWAY from the offices of Gem, there is a school. And where there is a school there are schoolgirls. And when the school bell rings there is break time. And when there is break time there are schoolgirls gathered in the corners of cloakrooms, playgrounds, corridors and toilets flicking the pages of this week's *Mirabelle*. And in this week's *Mirabelle*, between the Dollypops strip and a competition to win fifty quid's worth of fabbest Mr Freedom gear, on page 8 there is the uncanniest of prophecies.

'A New Year is upon us again and with it comes a brand-new male – the Super Guy of 1972. He's not going to be anything like his predecessor. In fact towards the end of 1972 he'll probably resemble a space astronaut.'

The accompanying cartoon of Super Guy '72 portrays a pretty young man in a space suit and knee-length platform boots with streaky coloured hair and make-up.

'The trendiest of males will be applying mascara and maybe a dash of eye shadow to their saucers.'

The bell rings. Break time is over. *Mirabelle* is rolled back up and crammed in a satchel. But the genie of Super Guy '72 is out of his bottle . . .

MICHAEL AND BARRIE BLINK. Before them, rising from a chair, stands a figure in a strange two-piece quilted futuristic jumpsuit patterned like an electrical circuit board. The collarless top is unzipped, revealing a bony alabaster chest. The crotch area is padded, the trouser legs turned half-mast to the knees, showing off a gleaming pair of fire-engine-red wrestler boots with thick platform soles. The hair, nothing like the sweeping Greta Garbo on the sleeve of *Hunky Dory*, is short and parted, spiky at the crown with ears poking out at the sides through pixieish bangs. Strangest of all, the eyes beneath the wispy fringe don't appear to match; one looks an insane scrutinising blue, the other a druggy dilated brown. The bangled hand that isn't holding a smoking cigarette suddenly extends. Michael takes it, shakes it and mentally readjusts. Behind him, the grin that's been on Barrie's face since he woke up this morning stretches another inch.

'Hi.' A flash of kinked teeth. 'I'm David.'

He sits down, mirroring Michael making himself comfortable in the chair opposite. Near the back wall, Barrie quietly pulls his Pentax out of his doctor's bag. David leans forward in his chair to light a fresh Marlboro Red, sucking in the flame before slumping back, holding it the way stole-swaddled vamps do in old movies: wrist aloft, hand palm up, wiggling it between index and middle fingers, letting the smoke curl up and away like a distress flare at sea. He swings a red-booted left leg over his right knee, the foot within noticeably twitching. He softly kneads his jaw. He puffs. He grins. He is ready to detonate.

4

David knows what he's going to say before any questions have been asked. He knew when he woke up this morning, ears pricking to the distant rattle of plates as Donna, sometimes more affectionately 'Dolly', from over the road began her daily clean of his kitchen. He knew last night when he fell into his four-poster bed with his wife, Angie, as their seven-month-old son Zowie gurgled in his cot nearby. He knew last Sunday, bumping hips to 'Mr Big Stuff' on the dancefloor of the Sombrero with his powderpuffed gang of Freddie, Daniella, Wendy and sundry sulphate courtesans male, female and all 57 varieties in between. He knew last Saturday when he turned 25 and destiny's bell rang a violent now-or-never *ding ding*. He's known for days, for weeks, for the past few months, the pressure building, his mind sharpening, his music hardening, his entire body electrifying. He just didn't know *when*. Until yesterday, when he was told *Melody Maker* wanted to meet him. His first interview of 1972. That's when David knew.

Today, it begins.

LIKE MOST DAYS FOR DAVID, it begins in the rented ground-floor flat at 42 Southend Road in Beckenham with a cup of coffee, a glass of orange juice and a 'Morning, Dolly' to Donna Pritchett. Mornings in Haddon Hall are a lot quieter now that the upstairs landing has emptied of its three lodgers: David's band, Mick, Trevor and Woody, have all moved to a rented first-floor flat two miles away near West Wickham station. As Donna dusts, Angie runs him a bath where David calmly contemplates the big day ahead surrounded by soap, shampoo and a pile of sex magazines for long soaks – *Forum, Curious, Heat, Club International* – while his baby son is handed over to the care of Sue Frost, their downstairs neighbour and on-site nanny. Angie then helps Donna tidy up the front room where a faint perfume of Lebanese smoke still hangs in the air over the strewn sleeves of *There's A Riot Goin' On, Roger The Engineer, Fun House* and *Chuck Berry's Greatest Hits*. Outside, in tandem, the landlord, old Mr Hoy, stoops meticulously raking the dead leaves from the front border like a figure in the background of a Constable painting.

Any other day and David might go straight to his piano room overlooking the giant back garden, its curly lamps and Lalique glass his mute audience to the first vibrations of 'Five Years', 'Lady Stardust' and every other song debuted between the walls still raw with the afterbirth of fresh crossings-out and sudden chord changes. But today, the day it begins, there isn't time. Out of the bath, he spends a necessary forever in his pink bedroom, zipping into the new clothes his dear friend Freddie made for him. A matching quilted cotton two-piece, cut from a grey-and-dark-green circuit-board print from Liberty's of London. The top is like a small windcheater, the jean bottoms inspired by Freddie's favourite designer, Antony Price from Che Guevara on Kensington High Street. Price has just launched cheeky 'bummy' pedal pushers for women with extra material stitched into the rear. For David, Freddie borrows the same idea but swaps it round to the front, creating an even cheekier bulging padded crotch – as if David doesn't bulge enough unassisted. To finish, he slips into his new red platform boots, made to order by Russell & Bromley. A last tease of his newly chopped hair in his copper-framed mirror, then he steps outside to the basement garage on the south side of the house, home to his three Rileys: the antique Gamecock, the black-and-grey one and the red-and-white one, which he climbs inside, turning the ignition. Mr Hoy, still raking his leaves, doesn't look up as David snakes onto the driveway and off towards the city.

So it begins.

Like a film, with David's car vanishing into the distance in a panning crane shot as the score trembles with the opening C major 7 caress of his new single, 'Changes'. His management have picked it from *Hunky Dory* as his best hope of ending the two-year drought since his last hit, 'Space Oddity'. The verses might be a bit weird, but it has a very Beatley pumping piano bridge recycled from his old 'London Bye Ta-Ta', and a big poppy chorus hooked on a stuttering lyric like The Who's 'My Generation'. This is why Tony Blackburn loves it. He's been playing it every day this week on his Radio 1 breakfast show; this morning, as David rose and bathed, it was sandwiched between the Faces' gin-breathed 'Stay With Me' and the soul-clapping 'Festival Time' by the San Remo Strings.

There's a very good reason Blackburn loves 'Changes' so much. Later this evening, the day it begins, he'll propose to his new girlfriend, actress Tessa Wyatt. She will say 'Yes' and tomorrow, after another breakfast show when he'll play 'Changes' again, they'll go shopping for rings. Hers will cost £300. In seven weeks they'll marry, the groom in a burgundy cavalry twill suit, the bride in cream wool with black knee boots, by which time Blackburn will finally have forsaken his Regent's Park bachelor pad for their new four-bedroom, three-floor semi on a private estate in St John's Wood. Until then, he'll keep spinning David's single as a dawn overture to whistling kettles, burning toast and soggy cornflakes for the rest of January. Like a conjugal mantra.

To David, 'Changes' is now just an old premonition he wrote six months ago, since come to pass in hair, cloth and sound. The song's fate in a pop chart currently topped by the New Seekers' 'I'd Like To Teach The World To Sing' doesn't particularly interest him. *Hunky Dory* has been on sale less than four weeks but, already, it's The Past. The clock has struck, the calendar flipped and the slate wiped. Today it begins. *It*. The Future. A new year, a new David.

'He's not going to be anything like his predecessor . . .'

'ZIGGY STARDUST.'

He says it between foppish cigarette puffs as Michael's pen skips shorthand across his spiral-bound notepad. David repeats it.

'The Rise And Fall Of Ziggy Stardust And The Spiders From Mars.'

The name of his new album, more or less finished, now playing in all its hard and sparkly near completion on a tape machine in the corner of the office.

He tells Michael 'it's about the adventures and eventual break-up of a fictitious rock group'. Apart from the odd 'cosmic' and 'spaced-out' in the old hippie sense of something out of the ordinary, he says nothing whatsoever about aliens or outer space. He has no need to. Ziggy is simply an archetype – 'a cliché' as he'll later put it – David's own Frankenstein monster, stitched together from strictly earthbound rock'n'roll flesh: the sad tale of the Legendary Stardust Cowboy, the wildness of his friend Iggy, the madness of Syd Barrett and the tragedy of Vince Taylor, the English rocker David met in Soho in the Sixties, so fried by acid he became convinced he was the Son of God. In the one song bearing his name, Ziggy is cursed by a similar messiah complex:

7

the ultimate teen idol crucified by his own vanity, like a grotesque caricature of a Jagger or Marc, his band, The Spiders From Mars, being an equivalent Stones or T. Rex. The rest of the album has no narrative story, just a collection of the sort of songs David imagines Ziggy and the Spiders would play, be it his old Arnold Corns rocker 'Hang On To Yourself' or Chuck Berry's 'Round And Round'. Michael is the first journalist to hear the album and the first journalist forced to decide where sonic fantasy ends and printed reality begins. Is he talking to the singer or the subject of the songs?

'I just don't like the clothes that you buy in shops,' says David, explaining his appearance. 'I don't wear dresses all the time, either. I change every day. I'm not outrageous. I'm David Bowie.'

He predicts he's 'going to be huge and it's quite frightening'. He believes he's created 'a new category of artist with my chiffon and raff'. He likens his work to 'talking to a psychoanalyst'. Michael scribbles down the answers to his questions, attempting to navigate the depths of the person who might be David Bowie from the shallows of the apparition that must be this new character he refers to as Ziggy Stardust. Possibly they are one and the same, ego and id, cat-and-mousing one another as much for their own flirtatious amusement as for today's captive audience of two, toying and teasing in a confetti of polari. 'The queer bit', as Rod might call it with a bra-unclasping cackle. Only this is different. Married and with a son, David makes no effort to reassure Michael of his throbbing machismo. Asked about 'Gay Liberation', the faint tickle of Sombrero champagne cheerleads his tongue.

'I suppose I'm what people call bisexual.'

And so it begins.

'I'm gay and always have been, even when I was David Jones.'

David smiles. Michael's biro skates across his pad as behind him a Pentax clicks. The Technicolor fiction of Ziggy Stardust becomes 35mm black-and-white fact.

THE SHORT JANUARY DAY of revelations is already night by the *Blue Peter* hour. In Fleet Street, Michael's fingers thunder upon the keys of his typewriter. In Dean Street, Barrie prepares his developer and stop bath in the darkroom of his flat above Pizza Express. In Regent Street, the bright shop windows down from Gem's offices do their best to defy a hurry-home dusk of black mirror puddles left by a day's drizzle and the damp-aired promise of more to come. But David doesn't hurry anywhere further than a few hundred yards down the road.

Heddon Street. In the cold after-work twilight when the pubs reopen, it's as lonely and mysterious as an Edward Hopper painting or the bourbon-scented nocturne of an old Sinatra LP cover. And so the perfect stage for Ziggy's equivalent wee small hour. Another roll of Kodak in another camera. This one belongs to Brian, the photographer who took the portraits for *Hunky Dory*, tonight primed to take fresh ones in the Mayfair side alley of fashion warehouses where he rents a studio.

David, still in his circuit-board suit and red boots, carries a red Shaftesbury Les Paul guitar. He borrowed it especially for this shoot from his friend Mark, Donna's teenage son who lives across the road. It's not the sort of guitar David normally plays but it is the sort he thinks Ziggy would play, and it's as Ziggy that David wanders in and out of Brian's lens. Smoking under the wrought-iron lamppost, inside and around its corner telephone boxes, snarling as he drops knock-kneed thrusting Mark's guitar, prowling the kerb of stationary cars glistening with rain like tombs of metal and glass, past dustbins vomiting too much unwanted rubbish onto the pavement in cardboard clusters. Until Brian conducts him to the chiaroscuro of a doorway lit by the electric flag sign of a furrier business.

K. WEST

David rests a boot on a bin, left arm draped over the knee, hand dangling like a sculpture by Michelangelo. His guitar slung to his right, he grips the neck, aiming it straight at Brian's lens like a rifle. Cocked and ready. His head is still, shadowed eyes gazing into the infinite beyond. The look of a man who can suddenly see his own future.

Only it's closer than you think, David. Much closer. It's already here, in town this evening, less than half a mile from where you're stood in the pissing rain as the Piccadilly pigeons fly. Down Regent Street, round past the Café Royal, keep on going, yes, that's it, all the way to the other end of Leicester Square. Now, do you see? Opening tonight at the Warner West End. This is the future, David. *Your* future.

Being the adventures of a young man whose principal interests are rape, ultra-violence and Beethoven . . .

TWO

THERE IS HIM, that is David, and his three Spiders, that is Mick, Trevor and Woody, sitting four in a row in the dark of the filmdrome, all warm and cosy on this chill winter bastard of an evening. It being the same filmdrome and the same bolshy whopper of a 43-foot screen where David sat not one year ago popping his glazzballs viddying Mick Jagger in *Performance.* And, right as dodgers, this icy nochy they're popping just as hard again, as he knew they would from the first slovo he read about *A Clockwork Orange.*

These past two weeks you can't pick up a gazetta without having the new Stanley Kubrick flick shoved in your litso. The redtops especially, all bezoomny and bothered about its scenes of naked ptitsas and ultra-violence, they say much worse than all that Hammer tit and fang, even though there's not much of the old red vino splashing about. It's a sort of science-fiction flick, set in an England of a future so near you can already smell it, about this wicked teenage bratchny called Alex and his nasty friends, that is droogs, who spend their evenings raping and robbing and scrapping britvas with other gruppas of evil little bratchnies, purely for guffs and kicks, like. Until Alex gets caught and thrown in chokey where he undergoes a radical new aversion therapy which turns him into a spoogy pacifist weakling. It's all a blacker-than-black comedy, really, making a very serious moral point about free will. But all the gazettas cry is 'THE FILM SHOCKER TO END THEM ALL'. Their biggest bleat seems to be they think there's a generation of bored young brothers out there who'll viddy Alex and his droogies and start mimicking their fashions by wearing boilersuits, collarless shirts, paratrooper boots, bowler hats, codpieces and braces with plastic brooches in the shape of wounds and bleeding glazzballs. What the *Sunday Times Magazine* call its *'futuristic skinhead'* look. And not just dress like them, but talk and act like them, what many fear will produce a copycat *'Clockwork cult'* of roaming gangs randomly raping, looting and killing as they howl 'Singin' In The Rain'. Which isn't such a far fetch when you remember that poor queer who got tolchocked to death by a group of stick-wielding bratties by Wimbledon Common two years ago. *Genuine* horrorshow.

Now, the funny thing about all this panic is that the bulge in David's new trousers was already designed, needled and threaded before he'd viddied a single frame of any codpieced droogie, not even in newsprint. But the inky sophistos from the warble rags, they're just going to assume. 'Tell me, art thou's kecks crasted from Alex's codpiece?' And David, being an oomny malchick, he'll just nod. 'Righty right, brother.' As it does him no harm to let them think he's all about the old in-out, synthemesc and rock'n'roll. For the same reason that this very nochy he's brought his Spiders to this West End sinny parlour, praying that *A Clockwork Orange* helps ease their rassoodocks about the new glad rags he wants them to wear on stage. Real starry snazz, like. Gold pants and blouson for Mick, shiny blue for Trevor, silvery pink for Woody, each with their own pair of bolshy wrestler boots in different colours, and maybe, hopes David, a light lubbilub of mascara. The trouble is that, being baptised in Humber water, they think if thou prancest around in satin platties and tarty lashes thou must surely be some faggy-waggy eunuch jelly, particularly Mick, convinced that his poor old em and pee back in Hull will be sob-sobbing in their cornflakes, creeching that their loving son has gone all bendy wrist and mincing gooly, 'Ee, what will the neighbours say?' and boohoohoo.

It didn't help the other week when David took them to viddy a ballet at the Royal Festival Hall, hoping it would stretch their gullivers to the possibilities of lighting, posing and putting on a show, like the outer limits of what a band of brothers might do on a stage. All magic flashes and costume wow. 'Fantasy,' David told them. 'People like to focus on somebody who they feel is not quite the same as them. There are very few stars around at the moment. The people, the groups, they're all so *boring*.' Only there they sat, all slurp and blerp with bottles of pop, and crink and crunch with bags of crispy-wispies, blinking their glazzies at all the lewdies in tutus and tights, slooshying all the pretty Russian pom-de-pom and sugar plum fairy dink-de-dink, but not much the wiser as to what *The Nutcracker* had to do with the banging yarblocko fuzzy wop-wallops they've been rehearsing with David. So come the hour, just a few nochies past, when they had their piccy-wiccies taken in their lovely new platties and booties, David was confused why they were still all kroovy cheeked and blushing silly billy, like thinking of the horrorshow paggering they'd get if they wore these fancies walking down Hessle Road or some such badger-arsed byway back in fishy old Hull.

But then, like in a fairy tale, David picks up a gazetta and viddies his first stills of Alex and his droogies, all scary cool and space yob, and reads all the raving burbles about Mr Kubrick's smashing new sinny flick. '*A perceptual experience coming close to being the visual equivalent of music. The violence and the rhythm of the film is the visual closest anyone is likely to come in putting the Stones on film. And this seems to go beyond the linking of sensuality and violence.*' And, eureka! Sparking up his gulliver like a 100-watt bulb, all hallelujah and bolshy praises to Bog or God.

'Come, brothers,' skravats David. 'Fear not thoust be woofy malenky sugar plum fairies. Follow me, and I'll show thee something dobby to put the swing back in your yarbles.'

So here they are, David, Mick, Trevor and Woody, flipping down the velvet in Leicester Square, right on the raz as 'NO ONE WILL BE ADMITTED AFTER THE FILM STARTS'. And when the lights go down, and the screen pops red, and their seats go all vibraty with the shoomy death march, their rassoodocks start to sharpen that this isn't going to be anything like *The Nutcracker*.

Welly, welly, welly, welly, welly, welly, well!

Then oof and crikey, there's Alex, fake eyelash like he doesn't know if he's a malchick or a devotchka, queer platties and bovver boots.

Ah! Doobidoob!

Then Alex govoreets and the three Spiders, well, they can't help but guff and smeck because, would you believe, he talks all parkin and bah gum, a proper Yorkie accent, just like theirs. Nudgie–nudge elbows David. And lo, and at last, they pony. Clear as an azure sky of deepest summer. These funny platties and licks of dolly paint David wants them to wear. Now they viddy well.

They're not poofy. They're *droogie*.

They'll look like a proper *Clockwork* cult, righty right. Like hard bratchnies in soft sweetie wrappers, all gorgeousness and gorgeosity made satin and boot leather.

And, oh! Doesn't it carve the zoobiest smile on David's litso. To see his three Spiders, now happy little droogies, goolying out of the filmdrome when it's finished, still guffing and trading 'great bolshy yarblockos' and hum–de–humming 'Singin' In The Rain.' Thank Bog or God for Mr Kubrick, thinks David. They're cured, all right.

THREE

THERE ARE THOUSANDS OF THEM. Frenzied and insensible, a savage mass of panicking hormones laying cheap-perfumed siege to a former skating rink in Boston, Lincolnshire. The first came last night, the rest arriving this Saturday morning by thumb, train and coachload, from Liverpool, Glasgow, Cardiff, Sheffield, London and every city on the National Grid between. Not one possessed of any reason, just the necessary 60p and a fevered prayer of joining the queue early enough to be among the first-come-first-served into the Gliderdrome's Starlight Room, risking cold, hunger and the strong likelihood their pilgrimage will end in the back of a St John's ambulance. None of which matters. Because *he* is worth it.

'*MAAARRRCCC!!!*'

The first T. Rex gig of 1972. Their first in Britain for two months. Their first since they were crowned top-selling singles artist of 1971. Their first since they swept the boards of the latest *NME* readers' poll with Best British Vocal Group, Best World Vocal Group and Best Album.

'*There's not been such a decisive victory since The Beatles were at their peak.*'

Their first since Marc signed his new deal with EMI who've just pressed a quarter of a million copies of 'Telegram Sam', the new T. Rex single out next week, anticipating it will be his third number 1. Their first since his new pal Elton John told the press, 'Marc's been a real shot in the arm for the British music scene – and my god did it ever need it!'

Their first since Marc, talking to the *Mirror* with as much modesty as he could reasonably muster, agreed. 'I'm a phenomenon. People need an idol. They've chosen me.'

A television crew is here in Boston to film the phenomenon in action, along with a coachload of journalists and photographers, all fed, watered and ferried here at the expense of EMI to provide glowing testimony in next week's papers. Among them, a young man with a Jason King moustache and his smiling sidekick cradling a stickered doctor's bag.

Michael and Barrie step off the press bus straight into a battlefield of Boots 17.

'MAAARRRCCC!!!'

The name is screeched, sighed and scrawled on forearms in smudgy felt-tip. Magazine pin-ups of his face wave above heads like semaphore flags. Some of the wavers start fainting before he's even on stage.

'MAAARRRCCC!!!'

And then he is. All 5 feet 4 inches of him, flailing his little arms aloft, in blue trousers, a gold shirt and matching gold lamé jacket, two perfect daubs of glitter under his eyes. He is greeted by a noise like 6,000 dentist drills firing at once. He boogies up to the microphone. He roars 'YEEEAH!' More bodies faint. He whangs his out-of-tune guitar as the luscious Mickey Finn fondles his congas and the T. Rex rhythm section trip into funky first gear. The kids, mascara-splatted Rorschach eyes and suckling mouths contorted in a thousand agonies of lust and longing, are too busy screaming to hear what an amplified mess the band are making. On the edge of the hall beetroot-faced coppers pant in their walkie-talkies begging for reinforcements. Limp rag-doll bodies are dragged from the crowd by nervous bouncers as crazed jiving fans accidentally knock one of the TV crew's lights off the balcony. It hits a girl standing below. Her collarbone shatters.

Side of stage by the cabaret curtains, jostling amid the press scrum, Barrie's lens follows Marc as he teases the front row within a fingernail's scrape of his Stratocaster. A sea of hands stretches out towards him; they could be raving, they could be drowning. Barrie's shutter clicks. A trillisecond of bedlam, forever preserved.

This time tomorrow, Barrie will begin another sleepless Sunday night developing and printing in an insomniac panic to meet the *Maker*'s Monday press deadline. Only then will Ray, the ed, make his final call on that week's cover. Whether to go with T. Rex mania in Boston, the split in King Crimson or some new Jethro Tull dates. Or that interesting piece Michael handed in on David Bowie?

'The expression of his sexual ambivalence establishes a fascinating game. Is he or isn't he?'

Ray ponders over Barrie's accompanying prints of David grinning with fruity mischief, bare-chested, cigarette in hand, dressed like something out of *Star Trek*, and decides maybe he is. And even if he isn't, as the first self-professed 'gay' pop star to come out exclusively to the *Maker* they'd be daft not to make something of it. But then again there's Barrie's great panorama of Marc conducting a sea of groping hands, and the inevitable screamer, 'T. REXTASY'. Or is that *too* obvious – a bit too close to what the rabid Bolan camp over at the rival *NME* might do? Decisions, decisions.

Ray pushes the bridge of his glasses up his nose.

Bolan or Bowie? Bowie or Bolan?

The office clock ticks. The silent presses wait.

On Tuesday, they roll.

Wednesday, it arrives in bundles of rich smudgy black on not-so-white newsprint, stacked like haybales in the back of vans driving overnight from Colchester. King Crimson get the headline. The phenomenon of Marc makes page 5. David gets the cover picture.

'Rock's swishiest outrage.'

There on the front of the *Maker*, bangled and bony-chested in his funny new space suit and splashed inside across page 19.

'He supposes he's what people call bisexual.'

And in column seven, the sucker punch.

"'I'm gay," he says, "and always have been, even when I was David Jones."'

The first copies leak out on the capital's Tube station newsstands that evening, racked next to the West End final of the *Evening Standard* with its tongue-in-cheek piece on 'Men's Lib' by the celebrated columnist and homosexual Angus McGill.

Thursday, it's slowly spreading through the provinces, grabbed up by its hungriest disciples after school or clock-out, read on smoky buses home to smokier terraced houses that tonight will throb to T. Rex unveiling the swashbuckling boogie of 'Telegram Sam' on *Top of the Pops*.

Friday, as tabloid and broadsheet alike mope over the latest unemployment figures, it's there on the shelves, waiting to be shoplifted by the country's now 1,023,583 jobless. So is this week's *NME*: the cover headline 'REXMANIA' beside a picture of Bolan on stage in Boston, which isn't nearly as dramatic as Barrie's inside the *Maker*.

Saturday, a good day for W. H. Smith & Sons where it continues to fly in the same pocket-money blitz as coconut cream T-Bars, beef Quavers and *Petticoat*, whose young female readers were told all they need to know about homosexuals three Saturdays ago: *'The sexual activity is somewhat unorthodox, involving as it must do some ways of sexual satisfaction probably never experienced by an awful lot of "straight" couples!'*

Sunday, the swishy image of David still lingers in the newsie on the shelves below *Titbits* as today's *People* dishes up the gospel of 'ME AND MY 3,000 BIRDS' by Jimmy Savile. Crumpet climbing in his bed while he's fast asleep and pinning him down, sometimes 'six at a time' says Jim – who's just been awarded an OBE in the Queen's New Year's Honours List.

Monday, the *Maker* lies thoroughly thumbed and tossed aside in bedrooms reeking of teenage distemper. Tuesday, it's down to the last dogeared straggler nobody wants to buy. Wednesday, and with the next armada from Colchester it's gone altogether. Old news, buried and – *surely?* – forgotten. Replaced by a new issue with Jack Bruce on the cover, racked afresh on Tube station newsstands next to the West End final of the *Evening Standard* with its piece on a new Chelsea boutique selling Teddy Boy fashions run by an ex-art student named Malcolm McLaren . . . but hang on! What's *this* on the same page, top right? Buried in the *Standard*'s wry round-up of strange cultural happenings from the previous seven days?

'A pop singer named David Bowie revealed to the musical press that he was quite partial to the odd bout in bed with his best friend (no, he didn't mean his wife).'

A LOOSE HALO OF SMOKE hangs over the bushy head of Tony Defries like his own pet rain cloud. The cigar that belched it billows between the fingers of one hand as his other pensively beats a pen on his desk with a slow steady tap, tap, tap. In front of him a telephone, an ashtray, a stapler, a manila folder, a torn envelope with numbers scribbled on the back, and a stack of magazines including last week's *Melody Maker* with *'"I'm gay," he says'* on page 19.

Tap, tap, tap.

Whatever grand managerial plan he had for David, this wasn't part of it. Defries didn't arrange the interview, nor hustle to get his act on their cover. He can't blame David's plugger Anya, as it wasn't her doing either. David did this all on his own with the bulge of his trousers and a gib twice as frisky. The *Maker* took as they found, and what they found was worth slapping on the front page instead of Marc Bolan. *'"Gay," he says.'*

Tap, tap, tap.

Defries takes another Cuban lungful and exhales a grey spectre, watching it spiral up and around his ball of fuzzy hair perched like a protective tea-cosy atop the fast and furtive brain beneath. Then again? *'Rock's swishiest outrage.'* If all publicity is good publicity, then the front page of the world's biggest-selling music weekly when you haven't had a hit record in over two years is genius publicity. It hasn't stopped the world in its tracks, but it hasn't stopped David's career either. The phones now tremble with more interview requests and ecstatic reviews for *Hunky Dory* continue their slow drip across the papers a full six weeks after its release. *'A masterpiece from a mastermind,'* says the latest.

No, Defries didn't plan it, but he can definitely use it. Increase exposure. Create demand. Build his empire. It's like Marc told the papers the other week. 'People need an idol.' The way Defries sees it, gay or straight, people need David. Or as Marc puts it on his new single: *'You're mah main man.'* Defries likes the sound of that too. Being the 'main man'. Yes. He likes it a lot.

Tap, tap, tap.

Bu–rum, bu–rum, bu–rum.

In another office just down the corridor, nearest to the reception of Gem Music, another kind of tapping. Not the taut scheming rhythm of a master plotter but the softer distracted tempo of right-hand fingers gently beating their worries on the vexed temple of Laurence Myers. Bu–rum, bu–rum, bu–rum. Laurence is an uncomplicated man who loves his family, Arsenal, Frank Sinatra, and his business, mostly in that order save the occasional cup final day. For Defries, anything is possible in a world of smoke and mirrors. For Laurence, everything is accountable in a world of facts and figures. That's what life, as he sees it, boils down to. Truths and numbers. The final score when the whistle blows at the end of 90 minutes. The amount of record sales needed to add another silver disc to his office wall. How many people would have read last week's *Melody Maker* in which his client David Bowie told readers he was 'gay'.

Bu-rum, bu-rum, bu-rum.

Give him his due, David had been nice enough to forewarn Laurence. 'Don't worry,' David reassured him, 'I know what I'm doing.' The figures on Laurence's desk typed on RCA headed notepaper say otherwise. One magazine cover, full-page adverts and giddy reviews across the board have not translated into decent first month sales of *Hunky Dory*. David's new album isn't anywhere near the UK charts, nor the US, where it's not even scraped the Top 200. The single, 'Changes', isn't selling either, despite the best efforts of Tony Blackburn. Not that Laurence blames any ill fortune on David's choice to tell one lone music paper which direction he butters his muffins. But facts are facts and figures are figures. The New Seekers are still number 1 and the self-professed 'bisexual', 'gay', 'spaced-out queen' and 'cosmic yob' David Bowie is still number nowhere.

Bu-rum, bu-rum, bu-rum.

Knock, knock, knock.

The door of Laurence's office pushes open just far enough for a fat head of dark hair to squeeze through. The head of a 27-year-old divorced father of two young children, attached to a body pushing its 5 feet 8 inches to a meaty 13 stone. A noticeably happy head with just a faint whisper of mania about the eyes, flickering with diet pills, alcohol and slumbering demons, and a joker's grin that immediately stops the bu-rum of Laurence's anxious fingers, reminding him he still has other irons warming in the hearth of UK pop other than luckless David.

For two years now this fat head and its chunky body have been bumping around Gem's offices, assisting one of Laurence's team of songwriter producers, Mike Leander, trying to get a break in the business without any success. But now that looks like it's all about to change thanks to a demo he cut with Mike before Christmas. Ever so simple – a heavy danceable beat, a shouty chorus and a riff so buzzy it sounds like it's being strummed on a live plug socket – but ever so catchy. At least Bell Records must think so as they're just sorting out a deal to put it out as a debut single. It means they'll need to go back in the studio and quickly record a B-side, but Mike reckons they can cook one up just by mucking around with the same tapes to create an instrumental version they can label 'Part 2' or something. If they can get it on the radio and in the discotheques, Laurence has faith it will be a massive hit. For his years of perseverance, Mike deserves it.

So does his grinning fat-headed office boy who'll be fronting the whole shebang under a new stage name. Well, most singers use them these days. Marc Bolan's not his actual birth name. Nor is Elton John, nor Gilbert O'Sullivan, nor even David Bowie. Which is why he's not going to be Paul Gadd anymore.

'Ah!' Laurence smiles with a beckoning wave of his hand. 'Come in, Pau–.' He stops abruptly, breaking into a light chuckle. 'Sorry, force of habit.'

Halfway through the door, Gary Glitter throws back his fat head and laughs.

FOUR

THE LOST LAUGHTER OF DROOGS echoes around the market square. Trapped in the cold glass and cruel cement of the surrounding shopping arcade, designed by the same German architect who for the last 15 years has been slowly suffocating the soul of Merrie England one concrete slab at a time. That's why the droogs were here last February. Stanley Kubrick thought it looked like the nightmare tomorrow Anthony Burgess describes in *A Clockwork Orange*, the sort of ugly functional futuristic thugopolis where Alex and his gang would beat up a professor carrying books home from the library. The scene was filmed, but never used, and the last anyone saw of a droog in Friars Square was the celluloid scraps on Kubrick's cutting-room floor. But the tread of their bovver boots still shakes the Gulag-grey pebbledash. Tonight, Aylesbury, the droogs are back in town.

They sit waiting across the other side of the square, in the upstairs dressing room of the Borough Assembly Hall, dressed in shiny golds, blues, pinks and Liberty's circuit-board green-and-grey. They are all nerves and nicotine, checking and rechecking themselves in the bulb-bordered vanity mirror. David, pulling up his waistband, careful that no ash from the Marlboro dangling from his lip drops onto his boots. Trevor, inspecting the lamb chop sideburns Angie's just helped him spray silver. Woody, still unsure whether the costume Freddie's given him is the wrong side of pink. Mick, sparking up a jailbird-skinny Old Holborn roll-up, shoving the circular tin in the back pocket of his gold lamé trousers before stealing another glimpse. He laughs to himself. If the fair folk of the Greatfield Estate could see him now.

''Ave I *really* fookin' gorra wear this?'

His fellow Yorkshiremen cackle. So does David, hearing it for the bubble of tension that needed to pop. Angie sidles over to Mick, grabbing his top zip, teasing it slowly downwards to expose more of the hairless chest beneath.

'Ger'off!' he laughs.

'YOU LOOK GORGEOUS!' blazes Angie. 'YOU ALL DO! JUST *FAAABULOUS!* THEY'RE GOING TO *ADORE* YOU OUT THERE!'

Out there is where all the Sugar Plum Fairy dust of David's months of preparations finally comes to settle. Aylesbury Friars Club. He was last here back in September, the last time he and his band faced an audience. As he still likes to tell journalists, 'We got such a great reception, it got us off.' That's why he's come back: to get off again. He's spent the past week rehearsing with the Spiders in an empty ballroom in Tottenham, playing as if before a phantom packed house. Not just the songs but the lighting, the moves, the timing, all of it costumed and choreographed as near as can be to David's own ballet gala performance.

'It's going to be quite outrageous, but very theatrical,' he promises. 'Quite different to anything anyone else has tried to do before. Something quite new. And it's going to be entertainment. That's what's missing in pop music now. Entertainment. There's not much outrageousness left in pop music anymore – there's only me and Marc Bolan.'

Just him and Marc. David read Michael's *Maker* report on T. Rex's Boston gig with awe and envy. *'Bolan posturing glamorously . . . a return to rock'n'roll roots . . . girl fans who scream their hot little lungs out at the front of the stage.'* Except he thinks he can do better.

So do the two struggling young musicians among tonight's crowd awaiting his entrance in the Borough Assembly Hall. A dandy drummer with shoulder-length blond hair, not unlike Mick, and a dandier singer with shaggy black curls, not unlike Marc, dark sultry eyes not unlike Sophia Loren, and a monstrous overbite not unlike a Victorian mantrap. Last night their own band headlined a gig at Bedford College. Six people turned up. That's why they've driven the 30-odd miles this evening after a day manning their own clothes stall in Kensington Market, for some necessary cheer and inspiration. Like most of the crowd they've read last week's *Maker*, seen black-and-white images of David's new clothes and read the words 'Ziggy Stardust' and 'I'm gay, and always have been'. Like most of the crowd, that's why they've come. Especially the curly one called Freddie; after all, he did name their band 'Queen'.

The house lights dim. Anticipatory applause erupts.

BOMP!

Suddenly a booming bass note.

BOMP!

A low electronic throb like the heartbeat of the ground itself.

BOMP! BOMP! BOMP! BOMP! BOMP! BOMP! BOMP! BOMP!

The stage is still empty but the show has begun.

This is not normal.

Normal in 1972 is watching the band saunter on from the wings and spend the first few dawdling minutes plugging in and tuning up.

Twang, twang, ba-doing, 'Evening!', plonk, feedback, wallop, 'Wooh! Alright!', thud, thud, thud.

It's what every band does. It's what Marc did in Boston and what David did the last time he played Friars. But that was then, before the new suits and boots of Ziggy Stardust And The Spiders From Mars.

DOOT-DOO! DOOT-DOO! DOOT-DOO! DOOT-DOO!

The music isn't David's, but a reel tape he's asked his soundman Robin to play as an entrance theme: Alex's beloved Ludwig van from the soundtrack LP of *A Clockwork Orange*, the fourth movement of Beethoven's *Ninth Symphony*, multi-tracked on Moog and vocoder by American electronic music pioneer Walter Carlos and his producer Rachel Elkind. Like the HAL computer from *2001: A Space Odyssey* singing in German above an orchestra of blipping pinball machines.

Lights start flashing above the stage as the dancefloor lurches into warp drive. The last longhaired bodies who'd been sat cross-legged on the floor yank themselves upright, mouths slackening, eyes widening. Slacker and wider still when David and his band march into view, an ode to joy in glittery cloth and glistening plastic, looking like they've just barged in, fully sharpened, straight from the Korova milk bar. The one reviewer here from *Disc* magazine blinks at the stage and commits legend to memory. As they'll print it next week, *'Clockwork Orange bovver spacesuits'*. Let history record, the droogs *are* back in town.

'Good evening. I'm David Bowie, and this is my music.'

The crowd know who David Bowie is but not *this* music. It comes in fast jabs and hard punches. Three blows to the head, left, right, left, straight into 'Hang On To Yourself'. Then 'Ziggy Stardust', its first fuzzy chord a wallop to the guts, David bodyblowing *'uh!'*s and *'yeah!'*s as Mick plucks notes of phosphorescent lightning. The few hundred gathered here wobble with every strike. Some of them will remember this night, this music, and the vision of the band playing it on the Borough Assembly Hall stage as the moment their life violently jackknifed direction. Like Freddie Bulsara: at 25 already the same age as David, watching him cavort through 'Queen Bitch' as he might gaze into a fortune teller's crystal ball, the way he lustily puckers and camply pouts, hips grinding, fingers pointing into space as a silver bangle slips down his wrist. This, he sees, is the future of the Seventies rock'n'roll star. Shiny, sexy, athletic music that sounds like the clothes of the people playing it: skinny-limbed, bare-chested and bulging at the groin.

A cover of Cream's 'I Feel Free' comes loud as a rocket blast, Trevor and Woody all thrust, Mick all flames, his hair, clothes and guitar blazing luminous under the spotlight as he screws his eyes shut ready for impact on Planet Hendrix. The cue for David to vanish into the wings for a costume change: off with the red wrestler boots and circuit-board suit, on with a loose silvery Indian flock-print shirt, tight white satin trousers and matching white boots. New clothes for yet new shocks to deliver. The still wet 'Suffragette City', with its 'droogie' wink to the *Clockwork* cult, banging and gonging like an X-rated T. Rex, shaking the same floorboards which seven years ago shook to Enoch Powell addressing the local Conservative Women's Advisory Committee. *Wham bam, thank you, ma'ams!* And 'Rock 'N' Roll Suicide', sieving words from David's favourite bits off the musical revue LP of *Jacques Brel Is Alive And Well And Living In Paris*, flambéed by Mick's arrangement into epic teenage opera, like Don Giovanni being dragged to hell through a 200-watt Marshall amplifier. As it boleros to its climax, David slides to the front of the stage, bending down and extending his hand. The squash of girls at the front stretch out with theirs. It's just like in that photo he loved of Marc on stage in last week's *Maker*. Which is why Angie gave him the idea to try the same, only go a step further: star and fan, touch to touch.

Tonight, David is only too touchable. Minutes after the encore, a steady trail clatters up the rear concrete stairs and knocks on his dressing-room door. Girls, mostly, from the local comprehensive, plus the rabble of innocent misfits who drink down the Dark Lantern, welcomed by Angie's Broadway grin before they nervously shuffle in and see David, moist with sweat and aglow with such satisfaction the cigarette smouldering between his fingers looks post-coital. The press ad for tonight had billed him as 'THE MOST BEAUTIFUL PERSON IN THE WORLD'. Up close, he doesn't disappoint. The girls perch on his dressing table like crows on a rooftop, swinging legs and biting lips, throbbing pink with giggles and questions.

'Where do you buy your clothes?'

'I don't. I have a friend who makes them for me.'

'Why do you wear make-up?'

'Well, I don't want to go around looking like a dead bear, do I?'

A few more scurry mouselike to the other side of the room, where Mick, the Old Holborn tin back out of his trousers and another tight roll-up between his lips, and Trevor and Woody sit beers in hand, bare-chested and half-dressed in their stage clothes. Angie looks on proudly as her fabulous boys turn on their best Yorkshire charm for teenage hot cheeks and batting eyelashes. Now, so help them, Hull, they understand the necessity of all this glamour.

So too the two converts currently rattling back to London in a green Morris Mini. Roger at the wheel, Freddie beside him. Minds blown. Bars raised. Challenge accepted.

MIDNIGHT STRIKES IN AYLESBURY. The market square is empty but the lost laughter of droogs still echoes louder than ever. The giant glass cafeteria like an abandoned spaceship crashed on top of the shopping arcade looks eerily even more so. The air is very cold. The sky is very black. The Milky Way is very clear.

'DO YOU BELIEVE IN UFOS?'

Is the burning question *The Sun* asks its readers three days after British soldiers murder unarmed civilians in Derry.

'*Have you ever seen one?*'

Yes, says Betty in Leeds.

'I saw a brilliant light stationary in the sky. Attached was a small blue light. Suddenly the whole thing seemed to burst and eject a red ball.'

So has Ian in Watford.

'It was a bronze-coloured shape whizzing across at incredible speed.'

And Mary in Liverpool.

'An incandescent egg-yolk-shaped object. No aeroplane noise. No navigation lights.'

And Mr and Mrs Hall in Barrow-in-Furness.

'Dome-shaped and grey, it was moving very fast, and yet there was no sound.'

And David in Soho.

'There's a . . . *da-daaa!*'

He is back below ground in Trident Studios, where he's been since last November recording the album he thought he'd finished two weeks ago. Only he's just been told he hasn't by a man sitting 3,000 miles away in a Manhattan office wearing chunky glasses, penny loafers and a turtle-neck sweater. The man who signed David to RCA, their Vice President of Contemporary Music, Dennis Katz.

When Dennis turns on his radio he hears Karen Carpenter weeping over willows, Don McLean bye-bye-ing on whiskey and rye and Melanie bragging about her roller skates. Then he plays the master tape of *The Rise And Fall Of Ziggy Stardust And The Spiders From Mars* and hears David crying about Armageddon, man-love, boys in make-up, rough sex and suicide. It's not so much what Dennis hears but what he doesn't. 'A radio hit,' he tells David. 'It needs a single.' And so David gives him one.

'There's a . . . *da-daaa!*'

He talks his band through the melody.

'That's the chorus, then the bridge bit. *La, la-la, la-la* . . .'

Simple enough for Trevor and Woody to learn in one pass, Mick already knows it from an acoustic demo he and David made at Haddon Hall before Christmas. Back then it was slower and folkier, the words only half-finished. David never mentioned it again and Mick forgot about it. So had David, until the request from Dennis. 'A hit.' David hasn't had one since he sent Major Tom into space.

Space?

Then he remembers. That other song he'd started about a man in space. Not a man sent *to* space but a man *from* space, a sort of groovy spirit in the sky, told with the same comic-strip simplicity as 'Space Oddity' and almost as gentle on rock'n'roll. Not a leather jacket of a song like 'Suffragette City', more a pair of corduroy dungarees – yellow or pink, with smiley-face patches over the knees. All light and sweetness, with two fat scoops of Judy Garland's 'Over The Rainbow', a tiny sprinkle of The Supremes, and a fat juicy cherry of Marc's 'Hot Love' squished on top.

The recording is quick, simple and over in a couple of takes. David listens back in the same control room where two and a half years ago he sat listening back to 'Space Oddity', his smoke mingling with Mick's sat alongside him, scribbling rough notes for a string part they'll add later. Even without it, the song sounds like the hit Dennis asked for. A cute and catchy four-minute Coke float for under-the-covers transistor dreamers. Wherever the stranded Dorothy Gales are in 1972, whatever her or his name, this will be their hymn of hope.

'Starman'

Of course, it'll mean, once again, changing the chemistry of *The Rise And Fall Of Ziggy Stardust And The Spiders From Mars*, bumping off the Chuck Berry cover and adding an extra element of sci-fi he never intended. But it's just a tweak of the running order, one good song David wrote replacing another he didn't. Otherwise, the album is still exactly as he told Michael from the *Maker* three weeks ago: a loose collection of songs about the adventures and eventual break-up of a fictitious rock group. Simple. The kids will easily be able to follow that. It's not like they're away with the fairies eating their sherbet-filled flying saucers from Woolies' pick'n'mix; or watching *UFO* every Saturday teatime to see Earth saved from aliens by peachy-bottomed women in purple wigs and silver boots; or reading *Mirabelle* where last week Marc was still banging on about his plans for a film 'about a cosmic messiah – a sort of intergalactic Jesus'. The kids of 1972 wouldn't be so daft as to mistake David's rock'n'roll 'Ziggy' alter ego and this new 'Starman' as one and the same.

Would they?

BOWIE 72

FIVE

WHAT COLOUR IS THE END OF THE WORLD?

Wreath white on the funeral cortege of a 37-year-old picketing miner from Doncaster murdered under the wheels of a scab lorry driver.

Weeping pink in the eyes of his four children.

Camouflage green in South Vietnam as a mad young boy lies chained to a bed because he fits every time he hears a helicopter like the one that killed his mum.

Blood red on the streets of Bogside where no amount of Fleet Street lies over who fired first can soak up the stains.

Blazing orange as a Union Jack is set alight in Whitehall by a crowd of 20,000 marching 13 coffins for the 13 Derry dead into the thin blue line blocking Downing Street.

Truncheon brown in the riot that follows.

And emerald green and studio charcoal, and elvish copper and satyr skin rose, and microphone silver and vampire tooth white, and East Riding gold and Steinway black, and metallic pink and shining snare orange, and circuit-board grey and husky-eyed blue. The Apocalypse arrives on a Tuesday night in full colour. Except for those watching in black-and-white.

BBC Two's *Disco 2* is dead, and in its place puffs *The Old Grey Whistle Test*, its new 'serious' rock programme for 'serious' lovers of fretboard

29

stench, presented by the droopy, but serious, moustache of Richard Williams, moonlighting from his day job as assistant editor of *Melody Maker*. Two minutes to 11 p.m. and cathode tubes buzz with the harmonica parp of 'Stone Fox Chase' by Area Code 615. Tonight's bill of fare: Jeff Beck, Gallagher & Lyle, Merry Clayton, Judee Sill, a 1957 clip of Brook Benton and the Four Spacemen of the Apocalypse.

Against the bare walls of a tiny fourth-floor studio, next door to the similar-sized cupboard used for the national weather forecast, David, resplendent, and his three Spiders, iridescent, mime to *Hunky Dory*'s 'Queen Bitch' and a rough edit of 'Five Years', Ziggy's two-and-a-half-million-minute warning of the end of days. Bad news never looked nor sounded more attractive. David, clothes like the Fantastic Four, head like Peter Pan, his voice bloody-lunged with doomsday urgency, singing it like he's living it with only a loose foothold on the precipice of insanity. One day, if not today, he'll finally admit why.

'I thought of my brother and I wrote "Five Years".'

Terry.

How many Armageddons has he seen, ripping through the concrete beneath his feet and the clouds above his head? How many worlds has he watched slowly disintegrate in little white tablets forced down his throat? What bogeymen still lurk in his aching chasm of a brain – or have the antiseptic angels of Blake ward chased them away for good?

The Cane.

He meets her there, at a hospital dance. A patient, like him, who might be crazy, like him, or maybe just epileptic, like some of the others. She is a once married mother of two who won't be having any more because the doctors have sterilised her. She is first to smile at him, and he smiles back, not so shy to approach and ask her name. She answers in a voice salt and vinegared by her native North East.

'Olga.'

Their first dance together continues into the following day, and the next, holding hands as they stroll over the hospital's daisy-dappled lawn. For the first time in a long while, since the earth first took fire and the heavens bled, since he last ran away and hid for days in a cave, since David told him he couldn't cope with him living under the same roof any longer, Terry is happy.

He and Olga are mad about one another but judged sane enough to marry. The ceremony takes place on a grey Friday afternoon in Croydon. He signs himself on the register as 'a clerk' aged 34; she, 'a domestic' aged 33. Their residence at the time of marriage is the same.

'Cane Hill Hospital, Coulsdon.'

Till death us do part on separate wards of schizophrenics.

But till then, a drinks reception at his sister-in-law's. Family, beer and kisses. He is wed, he is loved. He just needs one more thing to complete the happiest day of his life. One more body. His brother's. His half one. His only one. His famous one they sometimes play on the radio.

He'll be coming along later because he'll know. He must. Mum's here, and she will have told him. 'Terry's getting married.' And he'd have asked when, and she'd have said where, and that's why he'll be here. Any minute, coming through that door. 'Congratulations, Terry,' he'll say and then they'll hug and clink brown ale and talk about old times, old records, sax players, hard bop, *'woulda killed him if they hadn't drug me off'* and all that Kerouac *On the Road* jive. Any minute. After this bottle. Or the next one.

But until that minute comes keep drinking, Terry. Keep twisting off the metal caps and pouring it too fast so it froths and spills over the side of your glass, and smile at your bride across the room, and tell everyone how happy you are as you stumble backwards into your chair, with your collar loose and your blue suit crumpling and your cheeks flushed and your beer-sad puppy eyes mooning at the door like a dog to its dead master's grave. Because, deep down, you already know what that is, don't you? That dead black space, like the dull echo in your guts, there between the door frame you know he's never coming through. Oh, Terry – you poor sad mad bastard!

That is the colour of the end of the world.

THE LAMPS ARE GOING OUT ALL OVER BRITAIN. The miners who risk their lives so Prime Minister Edward Heath has enough voltage in Number 10's gramophone to listen to his favourite Beethoven symphonies demand a fair wage and safer conditions. Heath offers them a whole two quid a week extra. The miners tell him to stick it up his Ninth. Heath refuses to negotiate and a strike is unavoidable. The miners stop mining and start picketing power stations, blocking deliveries of coal and oil. Besieged by the pickets, their fuel stocks dwindle as the outside temperature drops low enough to freeze the fountain below the statue of Eros. Heath turns up the Downing Street thermostat and declares a State of Emergency. And so, one by one, the lamps go out.

The first on the Tuesday night when David sings his song of the end of the world on BBC Two. Piccadilly Circus is plunged into darkness. No Volkswagen, no Cinzano, no Coca-Cola.

A ban on electrical advertising isn't enough. Thursday lunchtime, the regional power cuts begin. Washing machines stop spinning, irons stop hissing, kettles stop boiling, ovens stop roasting, radios stop singing and *Watch with Mother* becomes watching a lifeless grey fish tank in the corner of the living room.

Friday – the day Terry marries Olga, the day *The Sun* christens 'GLOOMSDAY!', the day listeners of Radio 1 awake to the Medium Wave déjà vu of Tony Blackburn still playing 'Changes' – the government implement an emergency Three-Day Week. Makers of cars, shoes, baked beans or biscuits, the factories stop and the hours slash. That night, as Heath dodges the pelt of flaming torches from a mob in Liverpool, in Bromley the Odeon projector stops midway through *Straw Dogs*. All is darkness. The screen is blank, Susan George extinguished, the siege of Trencher's Farm unended. The Earth stands still.

In lucky Leicester Square, the projectors still spin. Giant golf balls, star-spangled majorettes, Pierrots, dancing dice, flowers that look like Barbara Windsor and all 6 stone 10 lbs of Twiggy shimmering in silver like the Spirit of Ecstasy on a Rolls-Royce bonnet. Just opened at the Empire, Ken Russell's *The Boy Friend* is where the choreographed wowzer of Busby Berkeley meets the pop art blimey of Mr Freedom. It's why Marc, who watches it on 40,000 feet of champagne on a plane to Los Angeles, names it his film of the year, and why trend-frenzied fashion eds prime girls to get set for *'a boop-boop-a-doop summer'* of head scarves, pleated Charleston skirts and flapper beads. But it is the only hot colour to be found in a week fast bleaching into coldest black-and-white.

Crisis day five and dairies ration milk to one pint less per doorstep per week. Bakeries can't bake enough bread and supermarkets start running out of battery eggs. Dentists are reduced to using foot-pedalled drills. Every day the fire brigade rescue workers trapped in lifts by sudden power outages and Heathrow passengers are forced to puff a sweaty half-mile from jumbo jet to customs when the moving escalator walkways stop moving. Sewage stations stop pumping and waste bubbles back up U-bends. Trains are cancelled and those that do run are freezing and overcrowded. Schools close and classes are sent home to depressed mums dishing up cold food in cold kitchens in a Jimmy Young-less silence. When finally lights flicker and the radio plays again it's the ballad of a man screaming *'I can't give anymore!'*

England, still shrouded in fog and ice, is told to heat just one room per house with no more than two bars of an electric fire. This isn't advice but Law. The penalty: three months in prison, a £100 fine or both. Heating is banned in shops and offices where salesgirls and clerks sit and shiver in their winter coats, scarves and gloves. Demand forces Tesco to ration candles to one pack per customer while the papers helpfully print tips on how to make oil lamps using bits of potato, dead matchsticks and cotton wool. Streetlamps and lights in high street windows are switched off. As in the war, after-dark pedestrians are advised to 'wear something light coloured or reflective' and, as in the war, some are accidentally run over. Others die suffocating in landslides trying to dig out old coal from disused railway embankments. Hospitals crowd with burns victims as camping stoves and candles become domestic death traps. Rapists thrive in an open season of women walking home alone in the dark and a battery transistor hollers *'look wot you dun!'*

Valentine's Day, and romance is scarcer than jobs. One and a half million workers already laid off and analysts warn there could soon be 20 million unemployed. The *Mail* predicts 'JUST 14 DAYS TO DISASTER' and the man from the National Grid cannot quarrel. 'The situation is grave,' he trembles, 'and as far as we can see it is only going to get worse.'

In these loveless hours of doom, gloom and candlewax, number 1 is Chicory Tip's 'Son Of My Father' with its space-fart synthesizer recorded for a flat session fee of £20 – two pounds more than the lowest miners' weekly wage. Those with power this Thursday evening can see them play it on *Top of the Pops* along with Harry Nilsson, all strings and suicide, and Slade, all stomp, wot and dun. Those who don't must make their own fun with tabloid tips of power-cut parlour games.

'*All but one sit in a circle. The odd one out finds a victim in the dark, sits on his or her lap, and says: "Squeak, piggy, squeak!" If he identifies the squeak, the two change places. If not, he goes to another lap . . . and so on.*'

What kind of dum-dum would move to a country like this?

THE DAYLIGHT HITS HIM like a baseball bat in the face. Grey daylight the colour of milky weak English tea, the sort of sky he's come to expect from this funny land of PG Tips, power cuts, pubs, Pan's People and goddamn 'pavements'. He rubs his squinting eyes, yawning in the just-gone-afternoon air spiked by the exhaust fumes of a passing 52 bus. He watches it for a second, weaving round the corner like a cartoon Mary Poppins reminder just in case he'd forgotten where he is, then steps down onto what he'll always call a sidewalk and heads in the opposite direction.

OK, London. Let's fucking go!

This, his new home as of a few days ago, courtesy of the splendour of the Royal Garden Hotel on the edge of Kensington High Street, until his benefactors find him something more permanent. Most of those he's spent trying to get his bearings, sticking mainly to the west, staking out Notting Hill and Portobello Road, checking out the clothes stores, the record stores and the foxy British chicks. He has the company of his new best friend who's been flown over with him, but his main mission is to make new ones. People to replace the something precious he lost back home, which is why he's come to England. A clean start in a new country, at least as clean for as long as he can stay clean.

He walks only as far as the traffic lights, waits for that funny little red guy to go green, struts across to the other side and straight through the door of Kensington Market. He's not looking for anything in particular. He's just looking. At the jeans, at the belts, at the shoes, at the hot hippie chicks selling them. Until he sees it, or maybe it sees him. Mutual love at first sight.

An American-style baseball jacket, made of leopard print and leather. The front is all leopard, there's more leopard in stripes along each arm, the lining is *green* leopard, and there's a label inside: 'Wonder Workshop'. Only when he pulls it from its hanger does he see the back: a print of a snarling leopard's head on a black leather canvas. 'Oh, man!' He doesn't have to try it on to know it's a perfect fit but does so anyway, twisting to admire their union in the nearby mirror. He catches the assistant's eye. She flashes a warm smile. He returns a warmer one of his own; a smile that could haggle the diamonds out of the Queen's tiara for a dirty Detroit dollar.

'How much?' asks Iggy.

SIX

MRS JONES, HEAD PROUD, STRIDE STEADY, leaves the foyer of her block of flats on Albemarle Road and steps westward in the direction of the station. It is a mild spring morning, the birches and hazels shaking their kitten-tail catkins in the light breeze as hopping blackbirds whistle cheekily among the privet hedges. Peggy wears her thick woollen coat all the same, her lipstick thin but precisely applied, her hair shampooed and set only yesterday with a chocolate kiss rinse sweeping up and away from her forehead exactly like the Queen. As always, by the same hairdresser at Evelyn Paget's salon on Beckenham High Street. That nice young girl Suzanne, the one she told Angela about. And it's thanks to Peggy that Suzanne now does Angela's hair too, and David's, and *thank God*! He looks *so* much better now he's had it cut short after all that silly business in the *Daily Mirror* about people thinking he was a woman. *But that's David.* Like all that other recent nonsense, telling some pop magazine that he's a . . . well, it's just not true, is it? How can he be one of *those* when he's married with a child? Peggy was so distressed she rang Angela. His *wife*!

Traffic lights pause Mrs Jones's thoughts. She waits, she crosses. They continue.

His wife! Yes. She's slowly come round to Angela. Well, these last two years she has been very kind to Peggy, buying her gifts and helping her furnish her flat. She seems to keep David's home in order too, even if she's not much of a mother. That Sue from downstairs seems to spend more time with Zowie than Angela does. *Honestly!* Her only grandson, growing up in *that* house, with all those queer friends of David's popping round. That thin young coloured girl with the shocking hair. Mariella? Daniella? Odd little thing, even if Zowie seems fond of her. Can't think why. And that Freddie. Now he *does* seem like a nice boy. Always polite to Peggy whenever she finds him there, usually sat at the dining table hunched over a sewing machine surrounded by scraps of cloth. *But that's David.* It's always been music and clothes with him. She knows he must get it from her. Quite something in her day. She always wanted to sing when she was young too. But then . . .

Oh, wait. Busy junction just over the railway bridge. Nothing coming that way. This way? OK. Quickly, then, to the other side.

But then? But then life went the way it did. Unmarried with a child at the age of 24. Now she's 57 and both her boys are married. David to Angela and Terry to that . . . oh, well, she's not right for him at all! She's been married before, that Olga. There'll be no grandchildren out of that one. It's awful, and both of them there in *that* place. Terry says they'll be out soon so they can find a flat of their own. But how is he going to cope? He says he's happy, but then look how drunk he got at the wedding. At least David wasn't there to see it. Terry says David hasn't been to see him in months. *But that's David.* She'll need to remind him about that.

Nearly there. Feels like spring, especially now the strike's over and the power's back. Horrible, sitting there all alone in the dark at night. And the *cold*! Of course, David never checked to see if she was all right. She might have frozen to death before he picked up the phone. *But that's David.* Fifteen minutes she queued for candles . . . oh, look at all these buds! Be summer before you know it.

Summer. Can it really be three years this summer? Three years a widow. It feels a lot longer. What would her John have thought of all this? Oh, he'd have *loved* seeing David achieve his dream after all the sacrifices they made for him. His dad would have been so proud, knowing his son was a big success in music at last, watching him on television doing his space song, and that other lovely one he made with Herman the Hermit. David misses his dad, she can tell, even if he doesn't say it. *But that's David.* He seemed to get on with his dad much better than with her. They both know that, even though she tries. But it's hard. They are so different, yet so alike. He has her eyes. The Burns eyes. The rest of him is all Jones, though. He looks so much like John his skull could have been cast in the same mould . . .

Here we are! The curving driveway. Up the stone steps. Press the doorbell. Angela should remember she's coming over even if David's forgotten. Mrs Pritchett might still be here too. The place would be an absolute tip without her. Nice Donna. A cup of tea and a chat about their boys. Yes, that would be lovely.

The door opens.

'HIIIIIII!'

Angie, face bright as the desert sun, cradles Zowie in her right arm.

'HEY! IT'S NANNA! SAY "HI NANNA!"'

She pulls the hand out of her baby's mouth and waves it with her own. Nanna smiles, her nose wrinkling.

'COME ON IN!'

Angie takes a step back and yells down the hall. *'DAAAVID!'* Then with as close as she gets to a whisper. 'Oh, but just *wait* till you see him!'

Before Mrs Jones has time to wonder what she means, her son steps out from the bedroom by the foot of the grand staircase.

'Hi,' says David. And grins at her like he hasn't noticed his hair is the colour of blazing crimson.

'SUZI DID IT,' says Angie, still bouncing Zowie against her side. 'DOESN'T IT LOOK *FABULOUS*?'

The smile on Peggy's lips stiffens and shrinks. Suzi? She means Suzanne from the salon who she introduced to Angela. The same girl who does her shampoo and set on a Thursday afternoon. Who cut David's hair shorter around Christmas time. Who last night came over to Haddon Hall and zapped it from the colour of a Kansas dustbowl to an Oz poppy field with the chemical magic of Schwarzkopf Industries of Düsseldorf, shade 'Red Hot Red'. Yes. That Suzi.

If Peggy was to speak right now and ask David why, he might tell her he got the idea from a Japanese model in one of his fashion magazines. Or maybe he'd admit he took courage from Daniella with her fluorescent white peroxide bangs. Or it might've been watching James Fox in *Performance* rubbing scarlet paint into his scalp. *"Avin' a laugh with my image.'* Just like David is with Ziggy, now sprouting the hair he wishes he'd have given him in the first place.

But Mrs Jones doesn't ask. She just stares and blinks at her son, the face of her dead husband gaping back at her with a head like it's been set on fire. Then turns away and hammers tight blue eyes on Angie.

'I'll put the kettle on, shall I?'

'**WHITE LIGHT AND SILENCE**.' It's all Max Wall says he needs. Tonight he has the light but not quite the silence. It isn't the 64-year-old variety veteran's usual audience, but better than last night's when beer cans torpedoed the stage. 'They told me if you like me you'd throw things,' he'd goaded, reaching down to hurl them back. The night previous wasn't much better. 'If you like me, you must hiss,' he'd said. 'If you hate me, then *cheer*!'

Mercifully, this particular crowd of lairy slugabeds isn't nearly so bad. 'Ladies and gentlemen,' smiles Max in bow tie, bumfreezer jacket, black tights and flipper-like shoes, his black mop wig slicked either side of his gravestone face. 'I shall now be walking up and down for you, giving you the benefit of my smile, sticking my bottom out for you, and you shall find it very attractive. Drum roll, please!'

A military snare rattles, and Max, as promised, begins to flop back and forth, grin set, chest forward, buttocks out, legs kicking epileptically. An infectious ripple of cool-losing laughter splashes around Guildford Civic Hall. Some of it David's.

It took him four hours of fussing to get ready for tonight, ensuring his new hair was proudly plumed the way Suzi taught him with the help of Gard anti-dandruff shampoo. Not for Max's sake, nor Frank the juggler, nor the sword-swallowing Stromboli, nor the Apache knife-throwing of La Vivas, nor the clumpy honk of support band Hackensack. David is here in full peacock, knowing that before the night is through he'll be aiming to impress the ringmasters headlining this 'Rock and Roll Circus' bill. The wildest live band in Britain today, if reports of the damage their fans wreaked upon the Albert Hall last July are to be believed. A band David's only properly begun to appreciate in the past year, who he's never met but just very recently reached out to, sending them an unsolicited package containing a reel demo with a scribbled message on the box.

A song for you to hear. Hope you ring sometime and tell me what you think.
David Bowie
01-658-1577

The song was 'Suffragette City'. David thought it sounded enough like one of their own ballsy rockers to want to record it themselves. The band thought it sounded enough like one of their own ballsy rockers to know they'd write better themselves. And so Mott The Hoople never rang. Not until a week ago.

'Hello?'

'Hi. Is that David?'

'Yes.'

'Hi, man. It's Pete from Mott.'

'Oh? Hi!'

'Listen, I know this is out of the blue and all, but I don't suppose by any chance you're looking for a bass player?'

David was confused. Pete explained.

Mott had just returned from a short European jaunt where their few fateful dates included a club in Switzerland that used to be a gas store. From the outside it resembled a giant metal pair of tits. On stage, the members of Mott felt like five more just being there. Three years of endless gigging, four unsuccessful albums, and for what? To end up serenading a few hundred Johnny Foreigners in a half-empty steel brassiere. It was the sort of bad juju singer Ian Hunter had been reading in his tea leaves for months. By the flight home he knew they'd no dice left to throw. The rest of Mott, Pete included, miserably agreed.

'You're saying Mott are breaking up?'

'Looks like it.'

'But . . . oh, no. Really? You can't!'

David was right. They can't. Mott's label, Island Records, are quick to remind them of their financial obligation to honour the novelty circus-themed tour they'd already announced for early April. Max Wall and the other support acts have been booked, ads placed, promoters paid and tickets sold. Weighing up the ominous contract-breaching consequences, there seems little choice. Mott are forced back on the road, sharing what they still believe will be their final tour bus with Max and assorted Big Top talent. The last fire-eating hurrah.

'You know what you lot need?'

'A hit record.'

'Yes, but what you really need is the right manager.'

A good point, thought Pete. Mott do, in theory, still have a manager. Guy Stevens, the frizzy headbanger who first auditioned them, moulded them, signed them, and christened them after a book he'd read in Wormwood Scrubs while serving out a conviction for drug possession. He also produced their last album wearing a Zorro mask, smashing up chairs and wall clocks before finally setting fire to the studio itself. It could be argued Mott could benefit from a little more stability in their lives.

'Like who?'

'Like my manager, Tony Defries. He's the greatest. He can fix anything.'

Had Defries himself attempted to sell the Christ-like miracle work of Saint Anthony of Defries he couldn't have done any better than David in his five-minute telephone hosanna to Pete.

'Whatever your problems, he can sort them.'

Two years ago he sorted the mess of David's career and finally landed him his deal with RCA. Now he's sorting out Iggy's mess, just signing him to CBS and flying him and his guitarist James over to London to kickstart a new Stooges. There's no reason, says David, why Defries can't help Mott too.

'Tony's the guv'nor, trust me. Let me have a word. I'll tell him you need his help. Then I'll bring him to see you.'

So here they are on a Sunday night in Guildford, watching Max Wall wiggling his arse as they wait for Mott The Hoople. Defries, a poker-faced mystery, Angie, a human fire alarm, and David, quietly anxious with the knowledge he'll be meeting the band later backstage. Pete was pleasant enough on the phone, but when he thinks of Mott he has this B-movie vision of a biker gang with guitars. Real hard cases, which is half the attraction, same as why he fell for Iggy and Lou Reed. David hates violence but he's a sucker for befriending any son of trouble who might otherwise smash his face in. Mott write tough tunes with macho names like 'Thunderbuck Ram', to be sung by men with guitars shaped like Maltese Crosses. David writes camp tunes with saucy names like 'Queen Bitch', to be sung by men with Liberty's fabric codpieces. They're both rock'n'roll, but they're standing at different urinals.

These are the thoughts whipping through David's head as the roadies clear the stage ready for Mott's entrance. That just because he's a fan of theirs, there's no guarantee they'll get on. In the flesh, he might find them much too yobbish. And they, in turn, might find him *much* too queer . . .

'**HANDBAG**.'

That's what the locals down the Black Bull call him because he always carries one. He is a he named Maxwell but he prefers to be a she named Michelle. She is 26, born in the Seychelles, and since moving to London has been in the dock four times for importuning. But to the first fireman on the scene who finds her, Michelle is just a body on the upper bedroom floor of a burning end terrace in Catford. The body of a dead trans homosexual prostitute.

Trannies and TVs. They used to be electrical appliances, but not anymore. Now they're ventriloquists. His name's Bobbie Kimber, he's 51 and he's built like a tug-of-war anchor man. He also dresses in women's clothes. As far as Hughie Green and the viewers of *Opportunity Knocks* are concerned, this makes Bobbie not just the hand up his dummy, Augustus Peabody, but also a female impersonator. Then he confesses to the *Sunday Mirror* that he had his 'inefficient surplus tissues' lobbed off by a surgeon in Morocco two years ago. He never told his wife at the time because they slept in separate bedrooms having long ceased relations. 'Though I can live as a woman, I can never legally become one, nor do I want to,' says Bobbie, who now has the full blessing of Mrs Kimber. 'He can never be a real woman in the sense I am,' she notes, 'yet he is obviously happier as he is.' But only Bobbie himself knows the unhappy truth – that he's still very firmly attached to his Brummie cock and balls, just willing to knock out a fib for the opportunity of whatever last drops of fame he can wring before the world forgets Bobbie Kimber in the time it takes to turn one grubby corner of a newspaper. And find another.

'SEX-CHANGE FOR TV MUSIC MAN'

The TV music man is, or was, Wally Stott, 48-year-old composer of the *Hancock's Half Hour* theme, orchestra leader and arranger of Scott Walker's first three solo albums, who recently melted his brass section by arriving for a recording session in a blonde wig and evening gown. Like Bobbie, Wally has decided he wants to live the rest of his life as a woman. Unlike Bobbie, he's been under the knife of Harley Street and is henceforth reborn as Angela Morley. 'I still call my father "dad" at home,' says her grown-up son, 'but I now use "her" and "she" in conversation with other people. Obviously, she doesn't want a big thing made of all this, but if she is to continue her career in music everyone will have to know and understand.'

Most people don't understand. Luckily, *Nova* magazine dips a delicate toe into the jacuzzi of confusion to try to explain. A transvestite *'is someone who gets sexual satisfaction from dressing in the clothes of the opposite sex'*. Whereas a true transsexual *'is someone with the physical characteristics of one sex and the psychology of another'*, the latter being *'a very rare phenomenon'*. Experts estimate the total number of transsexuals in Britain today at around *'550'*. Until the death of Michelle. Make that 549.

The fire didn't kill her, but the scarf used to strangle her did. The obvious mystery is whodunnit, and when. The 'who' will become clearer once the police surgeon gauges the probable 'when' so the crime can be pinned down to a finite time frame. The easiest way is a rectal examination: stick a thermometer up the corpse's anus and take the temperature. Rigor mortis sets in at an exponential rate, so how cold, or warm, the body is at the point of inspection will indicate how long it's been lying there and the probable time when life ceased.

This is all the pathologist dealing with Michelle's case needs to do. But he doesn't. The DI in charge has been asking Michelle's landlord and neighbours about the victim's lifestyle. They find out she was a he, a prossie and a ponce. They don't like to think what the police surgeon might find if he goes poking the long arm of the law up Michelle's . . . well, there might be, y'know, *evidence* up there.

And so Michelle's arsehole becomes its own protected crime scene. The temperature isn't taken so they can't know when, precisely, she was strangled. But they can always hazard a bent copper's guess.

They nick three of the little bleeders. Idle SE6 toerags making their own fun in a world of power-cut blackouts by setting fire to railway lines and sports huts. Young dumb arsonist droogies. They'll do.

One by one, back of the jam sandwich to Lewisham station, slamming metal against metal and flesh against brick. The longest night of their lives and sunrise won't end it. When dawn comes it brings only more darkness. Three bruised confessions to setting fire to the house where Michelle's body was found, and her murder. There is no lawyer present and nobody has contacted the boys' parents. They're 14, 15 and 18. Two of them cannot read or write, and one, a Turkish Cypriot, does not speak fluent English. The eldest, Colin, has a mental age of eight.

Their defence team gathers necessary alibis in vain. The police will make sure when the case comes to trial that they change the estimated time of death to suit their needs. With no rectal examination to contradict them, Michelle died whatever time they reasonably choose to say she did. Besides, confessions are confessions however they're extracted. The headline-sick general public certainly won't care. They'll know these lads must be yet another sign of our horrible times.

'AGE OF VIOLENCE'

Kids running wild with homemade weapons, screwdrivers filed to stilettos, knuckledusters and razors.

'MURDER FOR FUN'

That poor sod in Southampton stabbed just for staring at the wrong person; the last words he heard were 'What you lookin' at, mush?'

They're not even kids, these kids. They're animals. Thugs. Scum. And everyone, from the righteous *Sun* to the horrified Home Secretary knows why. It's these nasty sadistic films they watch. Like that story the other week about a jeering gang who threw a stone at a woman's car as she waited at the lights. They wore bowler hats, white trousers and boots. She said it herself.

'It was a nightmare from *A Clockwork Orange*.'

No, nobody's going to sob when the gavel bangs and these three little bastards go down. Three less *Clockwork* cult yobbos for the decent law-abiding folk of Lewisham to worry about.

And one less trannie poofter. Well, even the sentencing judge says so. In his words, Michelle 'has been no great loss to this world . . .'

SEVEN

WITH HIS OFFICE DOOR AJAR, the crack between the frame is like a
slit in a zoetrope forever amusing Laurence with its strange animations.
He never knows what they are, only that they must be heading to Tony's
office. Because they never look like the people who come to his own: the
label types, manager types, with their open shirts, eau de cologne, cufflinks,
cocktail cigarettes and invitations to Soho lunches. Normal pop biz people.
No, Tony's crowd look like they've wandered in to case the joint. Like that
little wiry chap last week with the leopard-skin jacket and silver jeans.
Funny name. 'Iggy.' And a funny face, like someone had surgically sewn
the top half of Buster Keaton's to the bottom half of Mick Jagger's. Very
charming, mind. So charming that before Laurence knew it he'd agreed
to let Iggy and his gaunt friend James move out of their Kensington hotel
and in to his unoccupied old home in St John's Wood. He's not exactly
sure how it happened but these things do when you're in business with
Defries. You end up signing a young man you believe to be one of the
best new songwriters in England today and the next thing they're sitting
in your office wearing a dress. It's like this shifty lot passing his door now.
Look at them! Buckled leather, sheepdog hair, hunched shoulders, dark
shades, clumpy boots. Who the hell has Tony dragged in this time?

Ian, Pete, Mick, Buffin and Phally: the five members of Mott The
Hoople.

The Guildford summit was a success. Once Angie broke the backstage ice with her sledgehammer of 'FABULOUS!' the rest took care of itself. Mott turned out to be decent blokes from the West Midlands, not a chain-swinging Hell's Angel in sight. David blinded them with his wild hair and wilder enthusiasm, Defries with sour cigar smoke and sweet promises. Formal contracts have still to be signed but already Defries has notified the press he's now their manager and David has agreed to produce their next single. As they understand it, he's written a song especially for them. This isn't strictly true. He's already tried it out with the Spiders but can't make it work, even if he knows it's still too good to waste. That's why he's offering it to Mott, and why they've all just traipsed past Laurence's door to Defries's office today to hear it for the first time, straight from David's mouth.

He waits for them, cross-legged on Defries's carpet, leaning against the wall with his 12-string guitar in his lap. Mott throw themselves around the office like clothes on a teenager's bedroom floor, their eyes loaded with expectation. David's left hand claws a C shape. He clears his throat.

'It's called "All The Young Dudes",' he announces.

Then he plays it.

AS DAVID'S RIGHT-HAND SWIPES DOWN, as his strings chime, as his lungs decompress, as his mouth opens and a *'Well'* springs out, as outside the window buses, cars, taxis, lorries and column after column of human ants hurry in every direction on the pavement below, less than a Mayfair mile away, just round the corner from Half Moon Street where David's rent boy friends from the Sombrero conduct their briskest business, in the government office of the Department of Education and Science there sits a 46-year-old woman busy at her desk with box files and a fountain pen. When not working, she enjoys gardening, eating lamb and peas, drinking whisky – if you can call Bell's 'whisky' – and watching *The Black and White Minstrel Show*. She lives just off the King's Road in Chelsea and has another house in the Kent countryside. She is married to a wealthy businessman, ten years her senior, and has two children, both attending private school. She is a Conservative MP who says she does not believe in 'class' and cast her vote in support of the anti-immigration policies of her party colleagues Duncan Sandys and Enoch Powell. She wants to reintroduce corporal punishment for young offenders and has reversed the previous government's plans to end separatism in schools and scrap the eleven-plus. She awards millions of pounds to fee-paying grammars as the inner-city comprehensives crumble. She is a 'FASCIST' say the placards of students whose union power she wishes to crush. So do the teachers, who staged a walk-out during her speech at this year's union conference after saluting her with cries of *'Sieg Heil!'* She is the least popular member of Heath's cabinet says the latest opinion poll, and the most written about say her average weekly press cuttings. She has cultivated an image of *'unapproachable remoteness'* says the *Evening Standard*. She is 'the open refrigerator' says the Labour Party. She is 'the milk snatcher' say the parents, a Lady Macbeth plucking the nipple from a generation of boneless gums, and few mothers doubt that given the chance she wouldn't happily dash their brains out too. When interviewed by a Sunday paper she confesses ignorance to the existence of the National Society for the Prevention of Cruelty to Children. Her name is Margaret, informally Maggie, but to the press she is always 'Mrs Thatcher'. In 1972 she is the Secretary of State for Education and Science. Which means hers is the raptor's grip on the future of every child in the land.

Which means they're fucked.

Suppose she could hear it right now, what would Maggie think of the song David plays for Mott? A song about today's kids, the same kids that it's her job – no, her *duty* – to nurture, educate and protect. Written in a language she wouldn't understand: 'dudes', 'jive', 'cat', 'boogaloo'. A Bowie song written in Bolan grammar, just like 'Back Off Boogaloo', the latest hit from Marc's new buddy Ringo Starr. 'That's how Marc speaks all the time,' Ringo explains. 'I'm a boogaloo, you're a boogaloo. Everyone's a boogaloo to Marc.' David's 'All The Young Dudes' is a similar highly contagious case of Bolan boogaloo flu, even namechecking T. Rex in the lyrics. But how would any of this sound to Maggie with her cold chemist's ears shaped for Mendelssohn, Rolf Harris and 'Telstar'? Is it remotely possible she'd hear what Mott hear, listening in awe and disbelief as, the more David sings, the more they want to physically rip words and melody from his fingers and run full pelt to the nearest studio? That this is a gang song for the gangless, an anthem of belonging for every kid who thinks they don't until the moment they hear 'All The Young Dudes' and realise *this* is their family. The kids who aren't all right because the deaf, dumb and blind adult world of career officers, coppers, clergymen and Fleet Street panic-pushers repeatedly tell them they're wicked, lazy, violent, stupid miscreants ripe for birching. The same as Maggie thinks.

But in Curzon Street she's much too far away to hear David's song. And even if she could, it wouldn't change one reinforced concrete atom of her breezeblock being. Just look at her now, in her executioner's twinset and dead white pearls, the embalmed smile on her sheathed dagger of a face, electric-chair eyes sparking with joy as she screws the nib back on her pen with thin, firm whiphand fingers. Another local education authority's proposal for comprehensive expansion scrapped, another good day at the office; hanging, drawing and quartering the helplessly poor, one rotten Labour-run borough at a time.

Others *will* hear it, though. Mott will make sure of that. Enough kids to put up enough of a fight. Because where Maggie brings discord, David brings harmony; where she supplies error, he supplies truth; where she gives them doubt, he gives them faith; and where Maggie fills with despair, David fills with hope. 'All The Young Dudes' is everything the otherwise doomed children of 1972 could ever wish to be told.

They are the future and all its news to carry.

IT IS ONE THING to give somebody a song, quite another for them to take it without asking. 'I'm flattered in the nicest way,' David lies to *Disc* but he can't fool Angie. She reads the angry silence in his pinched lips and tries to kiss them better.

'IT'S OK, DAVID! OTHER PEOPLE CAN SING ABOUT SPACE TRAVEL TOO!'

But the critics all agree.

'Like David Bowie a couple of years back.'

'With its parallels to David Bowie's "Space Oddity".'

'The same power and credibility as David Bowie's "Space Oddity".'

The jury is in. 'Rocket Man' by Elton John *is* 'Space Oddity' by David Bowie. Relit, rescripted, rescored and reshot. A Stanley Kubrick film remade by Walt Disney.

Elton isn't the real culprit. It's his lyricist, Bernie Taupin, who very convincingly claims his muse was a Ray Bradbury short story of the same name. Bernie's astronaut, like Bradbury's, isn't so much a tragic Major Tom, more a homesick family man in a future where interstellar travel has become as routine as long-distance lorry driving. But the coincidences in yearning mood and weightless tempo are too uncanny. Even if Bernie wasn't aware when sat at his typewriter, nor Elton as he tickled the tune of Lennon's 'Imagine' inside out on a Steinway, their producer, Gus Dudgeon, must have been twiddling the knobs with a déjà vu stabbing his memory like a throbbing wisdom tooth: three years earlier he also produced 'Space Oddity'.

The last Friday in April, 'Rocket Man' climbs purposefully up a chart where number 1 is a public execution of 'Amazing Grace' by bagpipe firing squad, by name the Pipes and Drums and the Military Band of the Royal Scots Dragoon Guards (Carabiniers & Greys). The papers are full of striking dockers and exotic fashions inspired by the British Museum's Tutankhamun exhibition. The cinemas are full of the guns, blood and tits of *Dirty Harry* and *Vampire Circus*. Tonight's television choices are *The Liver Birds*, *Budgie*, the final of *Come Dancing* and updates on the return of the *Apollo 16* crew who yesterday plonked safely back in the Pacific after 265 hours in space. Today, the day when David releases 'Starman'.

Today, the day when Elton meets a Starman. His name is Al Worden, the Command Module Pilot of NASA's previous moon mission, *Apollo 15*. Like a lot of *Apollo* astronauts, Al took pre-recorded mix tapes of his favourite music up into space: in his case, Frank Sinatra, Simon & Garfunkel, Judy Collins, the Beach Boys and Elton John. As a publicity stunt to promote 'Rocket Man' on his latest tour of the States, Elton, his band, assorted record company executives and attendant photographers are guests at NASA's Manned Spacecraft Center in Houston where Al, being one of only three human beings to have heard Elton's music floating in a tin can far above the world, is his personal tour guide. The cameras flash and the newspaper captions about one rocket man to another write themselves. As special mementos, Al presents him with an *Apollo 15* insignia patch and a photo autographed by himself and his fellow crew members.

'Thank you,' blushes Elton. 'I'll frame it.'

And he does, in another three weeks when he returns to the bungalow mansion in Surrey he's named 'Hercules', same as his middle stage name, after the horse in *Steptoe and Son*. At £50,000 the property is valued only slightly higher than Maggie's house in Chelsea. It comes with a heated swimming pool kept at a regular 95 degrees Fahrenheit, complete with night lights, and enough parking space for his five cars: a Mini GT, a Daimler, a Mercedes, a lilac Bentley and a Rolls-Royce sprayed metallic amethyst fitted with an in-car cassette player so he can laugh along to tapes of Monty Python. It's there, in Hercules's loft games room with its table football, fruit machine, ping pong table, golf balls and putter, vintage jukebox and life-size cardboard cut-out of Elton in an embroidered western Nudie suit with a dartboard where his head should be, that he finds space on the wall to hang his astronauts' autographs. Somewhere between his own gold records and a silver disc of someone else's: 'Jeepster' by T. Rex. A 25th birthday present from his pal and frequent house guest, same as the 20-foot cardboard cut-out of Marc last seen on stage at T. Rex's recent sell-out concert at Wembley Empire Pool. 'I think Marc is probably my best friend as far as other stars go,' says Elton. 'In fact he's my only friend. I don't mix with anyone else, really.'

This is true, more or less. He shares Hercules with just two dogs – Brian, a spaniel, and Bruce, an Alsatian – and his Scottish manager, John. He is also Elton's lover. As David might say, Elton is gay and always has been, even when he was Reg Dwight. But these domestic circumstances make it much less easy for him to say it in public. It's why Elton, unlike David, must suffer the rack and pincers of the *News of the World* until he can satisfy their curiosity why he's yet to marry. 'I'm looking for the right girl,' he grins weakly. 'I'll probably pick someone who works behind the counter at Woolworths, or Marks & Sparks where I go to buy my pants.'

For now, Elton's sex life is nobody's business, and while that remains the case he remains big business in a world of straight dollars and unbending cents. In America, 'Rocket Man' will soar as high as number 6 while its parent album, *Honky Château*, will be his first to smash US number 1. Back home, both peak at number 2 – his highest UK positions to date – if all too frustratingly kept off the top of *both* charts by the same artist. Anybody else, and Elton might mind. But how can he when it's his only friend?

EIGHT

SIPPING COGNAC AND COKE, Marc casts his spells on Fleet Street. 'It's ironic, really, being called a male sex symbol when I'm prettier than most chicks.' He smiles a choirboy smile of perfect neat little teeth, shiny white with fizz and brandy sweetness. 'Sure, I often get accused of being a queer, a fag, but I'm not. *Sorry, boys!* Actually I find it very easy to be turned on sexually by people, any people. But I just prefer chicks, that's all.' The flushing woman from the *Sunday Mirror* crosses a skirted leg. 'I've checked out "the other scene" but it just doesn't get me off,' he expands. 'So when some guy comes up to me and says, "Marc, are you a fag?" nothing happens to me inside. It doesn't affect or concern me at all. Usually I just say, "Sorry, sweetie, I'm too expensive," or "You're not pretty enough, dear."'

Prettier than most chicks and none prettier to most chicks. School days and weekends, morning, noon and night, they hover outside his flat in Clarendon Gardens, on walls, by railings, behind plane trees and on the bonnets of parked cars like expectant pigeons waiting to swoop on the briefest visible crumb of Marc Bolan. How they know where to find him is a mystery. The papers only mention vaguely that he lives in 'Little Venice, Maida Vale'. But they do, and the more that do the more that come. By train from Kent, by thumb and car from Hertfordshire, by Tube from the outer reaches of Metroland. They write messages on the wall by the gate, curving giant hearts inset with love spelled 'LUV' beside his name and theirs. They rake through his dustbins like archaeologists desperately seeking any scrap of documentary evidence to prove that he genuinely exists. They live on hope and patience and crisps. Occasionally, they see his wife, June, alone, spying her with murderous adolescent eyes hissing like swans. And, maybe, if life behaves as the romance strips in *Romeo* and *Mirabelle* tell them it should, they will see him, if only in the panicked bolt from the back of a white Rolls-Royce to a slammed front door. Their magic prince, robed in citric lime satin and cherry velvet. And he will see them, in their best stripey Dorothy Perkins. And they will hit the pavement like they've just been shot.

Number 1 in their hearts and their charts, Marc has done what nobody's been able to do for five desperate weeks of sporraned misery: deliver us from the evil of the Pipes and Drums and the Military Band of the Royal Scots Dragoon Guards (Carabiniers & Greys). The battles of Waterloo, Balaklava and the Somme they could withstand, but not the heavy doo-wop artillery of 'Metal Guru'. Like the ringing of Christmas bells in a blizzard of teenage spit and Woolies glitter, this is the tune pumping through kids' veins the week of two separate marches on Trafalgar Square by thousands of mobilised truants. The same week Mott The Hoople are in a studio in Barnes recording 'All The Young Dudes' with David. So the revolt begins. Kids waving 'NO TO THE CANE' placards, chanting 'WE WANT A RIOT!', some burning their school ties and blazer badges, others shin-kicking their way out of harassed coppers' headlocks, arms flailing in double V-signs like two-pronged rakes. 'Metal Guru' isn't about any of this – ask Marc and he'll tell you it's about the nature of God and why he doesn't need a telephone – but its primal scream sounds like a goal-winning *'fuck off!'* to uniforms, to homework, to six of the best, to Maggie, to the Pipes and Drums and the Military Band of the Royal Scots Dragoon Guards (Carabiniers & Greys). A very bad week for the stewed prunes at the *International Times* to run a cover asking 'BOLAN: WHO NEEDS HIM?' Here's your answer, hippies: an air-punching armada in elasticated S-belts.

In the last 12 months T. Rex have sold 14 million records. Not just top of the hit parade, as Marc tells Elton, 'I *am* the hit parade!' His old record label, Fly, repackage the first two bong'n'bongo Tyrannosaurus Rex albums from 1968 as one double: it reaches number 1. They do the same with the joss-sticky old single 'Debora': it reaches number 7. They follow it with a pick'n'mix of previous singles, B-sides and album tracks, rushed out in a cheap-looking sleeve called *Bolan Boogie*: it becomes Marc's third number 1 album. Other labels who've forgotten they had rejected Marc demos from the mid-Sixties mildewing in their broom cupboards suddenly begin wiping them off to claim whatever stake they can in the any-old-Bolan gold rush. Dubious PO Box ads for Marc T-shirts, vests, badges, patches, posters and Terylene pillowcases swell the back pages of the pop weeklies. Some genius in the employ of D. C. Thomson & Co reinvents the *Jackie* pin-up by splitting three double-page spreads over three consecutive issues to make up one ginormous six-panelled poster. Week one: Marc's legs! Week two: Marc's torso! Week three: Marc's head! Every lickable square inch more fantasy fuel to the gangs of praying mantises still sheepishly munching Chipitos outside his front gate.

Marc understands why they're there. It's all science fiction to them. He is somebody who lives in a television. They come to see him outside his box and it's like going to the moon. Nothing is real, and they don't want it to be, which is why they stand there, idly dreaming of the goings-on behind his balcony windows; whether he's writing poetry in the bath, or sitting in his yellow dungarees playing his guitar, or feeding his pet mouse, Boink.

Or the best part of three miles away across town in the new Bloomsbury HQ where he conducts most of his interviews these days, just over the road from where Charles Dickens wrote *Oliver Twist*. The office is managed by a stylish Giacometti-thin woman with dark red hair, bright painted red eyelids and two Yorkshire terriers, Rover and Daz, who have as much of a reign of the building as Marc does. Her name is Chelita Salvatori, formerly Chelita Secunda, formerly wife of Tony Secunda, formerly manager of T. Rex until Marc got rid of him the week after his recent euphoric Wembley shows where, even the critics agreed, Bolanmania finally ate Beatlemania and picked its teeth with the bones. Chelita was responsible for the first sparkles on Marc's cheeks. Now she supplies the ones up his nostrils. Stylist, dealer, secretary and confidante, her official title is 'Personal Assistant'. Marc's wife June has no need for suspicion. Chelita has been her best and loyalest friend for years. She's also much too busy shagging Mickey Finn.

Extra clerical help is provided by Marc's bassist, Steve, as runaround messenger, and 'Beep' as everyone knows B. P. Fallon, an actual life-sized Irish leprechaun who controls Marc's publicity. Control as in saying 'yes' to anything that rolls off an inked press, ensuring such maximum saturation that one week Marc is interviewed in four of the five main pop weeklies; the one where he isn't, *Record Mirror*, sticks him on the cover anyway as bait for a page four news story. Less is more but more is Marc, and the more who come to Doughty Street to interview him the merrier. All are led up the same stairs to the same room where Marc sits with his back to the same window, his ringlets glinting in the same sun, sniffing the same sniffs, sipping from the same glass of cognac and Coke, jiving the same jive about fame and fans and T. Rex's lack of any serious competition. How he knows what Dylan means when he said he feels 'pinned against the wall by millions of invisible people'. How rock'n'roll has given him so much but taken what is irreplaceable. 'Like if you take acid it burns out brain cells and they don't regrow. Rock'n'roll is like that.' How six months ago he thought he might end up in an asylum but now, sniff, he's cool with it all. 'The one thing nobody can say to me is that I'm not a true artist, man, because I KNOW I am. There's no way they can alter that fact by slagging me off.' And why he's reached the conclusion he doesn't need a manager anymore.

'One needs advisers, which is a very different thing,' he says over the constant ringing of telephones and yapping of Rover and Daz. 'Managers should be somebody employed by the group and getting a smaller percentage than the group. I don't believe in managers. All managers want to be rock stars for a start . . .'

TONY DEFRIES LEANS BACK in his chair and waits for an answer. The muscles around his lips dare him to smile. It was a good question.

'Would you have any objection to telling journalists to fuck off?'

The young man on the other side of his desk is smiling too. 'No,' he says. It's the right answer.

'Even if they're friends of yours?'

'No.' A shake of the head. 'No, not really.'

'Good,' nods Defries. 'That's settled, then. How much do you want?'

'You mean wages?'

'Yes.'

'A week?'

'Yes.'

'Oh . . . I dunno. Thirty, forty quid?'

The telephone on his desk starts to ring. Defries ignores it. He pauses just long enough for effect. 'I'll pay you seventy,' he says, warm as a fresh scone. 'But for that I expect you to work twice as hard.'

He stretches out a hand. Dai Davies shakes it and David Bowie has a new public relations man.

It was David who recommended him. He's known Dai for over a year as the boyfriend of Anya, his tireless Northern angel of a plugger. Dai is Welsh, not that anyone who hears his full name ever need ask. Big as a Swansea scrum half, voice soft as the foamy waves lapping the bible-black rocks of Carmarthen Bay. A voice that isn't afraid to say 'fuck off' to pesky scribes from *Record Mirror*. Dai knows the machinations of the press, having written bits and bobs for the defunct *Music Now* and the odd business piece for the *NME*. He also knows the machinations of publicity, having worked for top PR man Tony Brainsby when he used to look after Mott The Hoople. Dai's biggest claim to media infamy is that, with the group's blessing, he stoked the outrage after last summer's Albert Hall gig by ringing up tabloids pretending to be an aggrieved punter who'd gone 'thinking Mott The Hoople was an operatic programme' but left aghast at the 'vandalism'. The price was Mott getting banned. The reward was Mott getting headlines. Dai is exactly the sort of person Defries needs in his command. The good book tells him as much.

'There is another level of show business that transcends economic success. That's media success, media power. What Presley has, thanks to the Colonel, is the most media power he could possibly have.'

Media power. So it is written in the good book.

'The Colonel doesn't sell Elvis to the public. He sells Elvis to the people who sell to the public . . . the media people . . . Elvis, as a product, always is in the state of being sold.'

Always being sold. So it is written in the good book.

'Let someone else (RCA) pick up the expensive overhead.'

Let RCA pick up the expense. So it is written in the good book.

'You can make your own rules as long as you can get away with it and that's what makes a good manager.'

Make your own rules and get away with it. Amen.

Defries's holy scripture is *Elvis*, the first major biography of The King by *Rolling Stone* writer Jerry Hopkins; not yet published in Britain, it's already a bestseller in America where he picked up the copy that's been corner-folded, underlined and in places committed to memory. Like it's an instruction manual called *How to Manage a Superstar* by Colonel Tom Parker.

Complete control. That's the secret of the Colonel's genius. That's why Elvis is Elvis. He exists only on record, on screen, in photographs, on stage, on T-shirts, on badges, on hats, on scarves, on watches, on bedding, on lunch boxes, on the shittiest plastic tat that ever had the letters E, L, V, I and S stamped on its surface. And the Colonel owns every note, frame, negative, ticket, thread and injection-moulded atom of it.

As Hopkins spins the familiar fairy tale, once upon a time there was a young boy who could sing named Elvis Presley. Then he met the magic Colonel who turned him into an ELVIS. To Defries, this is the kernel of the Colonel. You take a boy who can sing called David Bowie and you turn him into a BOWIE. Only for David to become like Elvis, untouchable, Defries must become more like the Colonel, unfuckable. Never settle for their last offer when you can squeeze them for one more dollar. Never pick up the cheque when someone else can. Increase demand by suffocating supply: the fewer interviews, the greater the interest. Make the press beg for 'yes' by always telling them 'no'. Never let the public see the star off their pedestal: the less they do, the brighter the star, the higher the pedestal. And remember your artist is a product that must be kept, always, in a constant state of being sold.

Media is power. Power is success. Success is money.

This is why he's hiring Dai. To implement Operation Fuck Off. Enough of reporters ringing David at random to grab a quote for their readers' questions page about what make of saxophone he plays on *Hunky Dory*. Or unsupervised home visits like Rosalind from *Disc*, back at Haddon Hall last week with a photographer who snapped David on a stepladder while he painted his living-room ceiling. A stepladder is not a pedestal. A superstar is not a decorator. From now on David won't be allowed to burp at a journalist without prior clearance from Defries. His fixed objective is the same as the Colonel's: complete control.

But to get it Defries knows he must get out: physically, from the offices of Gem; financially, from his partnership with Laurence. When he came to him two years ago, a lone legal clerk looking for a foothold in the management business, he only had David. Now, thanks to the shelter of Gem, he's built up a roster: David, still his priority; his one-time bosom companion Dana, still unsigned; Iggy, still to make a new record; and Mott The Hoople, still to return any of his contracts with their signatures. The bottom line is it's still Laurence's company and Defries is still just a junior partner. As long as he stays one, then David and Iggy and Mott and anyone else he chooses to sign – however cool, sexy and exciting – will still be part of the same organisation as Gary Glitter.

'*Gary Glitter (I just love that name) has come up with a record with the title "Rock And Roll (Parts 1 & 2)" which apart from the grunted non-vocal and apparent(ly?) ripped-off Bolan riffs is so contrived that with enough exposure it could be a surprise hit.'*

Along the corridor, Laurence gazes fondly at the *NME* spread across his desk. Good old Roy Carr. He couldn't agree more. '*With enough exposure.'* That's been Gary's big obstacle so far. The discotheques are playing it, but it's not getting on the radio. The same goes for David. Take 'Starman'. The reviews have been incredible. '*If this record is overlooked it will be nothing less than stark tragedy,'* wrote John Peel. But the airplay has been slow. Only a couple of spins on Tony Blackburn in its first month, a few on Johnnie Walker, and Anya promises she's still working on Dave Lee Travis. But when he thinks about those latest account figures . . . how much have they spent on David now? About £29,000, wasn't it? Thirty grand. *Deficit.* Christ! That's three Rolls-Royce Silver Shadows' worth!

Tony doesn't seem to notice, but then he never does. It's spend, spend, spend with Tony, good money after bad. And every penny of it Laurence's. If this next *Ziggy* LP thing doesn't pay dividends, then . . . *God knows.* Doesn't bear thinking about. Like Arsenal losing the FA Cup to bloody Leeds United. And only fifth in the league . . . Still, upwards and onwards, Laurence. Those plans to launch your own record label for budget compilations are coming together very nicely. Brilliant idea, too. So simple! Original tracks by original artists, not like those cheap soundalike *Top of the Pops* ones with dolly birds on the cover. And you've just taken on the New Seekers on the' back of their second place in this year's Eurovision. And there's still hope for Gary. *'I just love that name.'* Wonder if he's seen this week's *NME* yet? Must show him when he next pops . . .

Knock, knock, knock.

Laurence looks up at his door. 'Come in.' It gently pushes open and a black bushy head pokes round.

It isn't Gary's.

'Laurence?' smiles Defries. 'Have you got a minute? Something quite important I'd like to discuss with you . . .'

NINE

EVERYTHING CHANGES. In the space of 24 hours, the blink of a bloodshot eye and the roar of a jet engine. One minute David's on stage looking out over a half-empty town hall in Middlesbrough. The next he's in a chauffeured limousine, staring at the approaching Manhattan skyline on his way to see Elvis Presley in concert. Is this actually happening?

'. . . *listening to WABC on this very special Elvis night! New York welcomes the King of Rock'n'Roll in person! Tonight, tomorrow and Sunday at the Garden . . .*'

It is. Clear as the voice on the radio. Clear as the inside of a diamond. The dwarfing twin towers of the new World Trade Center, like a pair of monoliths from *2001: A Space Odyssey*. The Empire State Building syringing the sky, its tip casting eternal hallucinations of a giant ape swatting fighter planes. The smell of perfume and smoke. Some of it his. The rest of it wafts from the pores and lips of his three companions. Angie, powderpuff dabbing her face like a mosquito. Mick, Cadillac-eyed cooing at 'the size of summa the kaaz' in the accent he smuggled through customs. Defries, quietly checking his watch as they bump through evening traffic over the Queensboro Bridge. These, the three heroes in David's life. His scarecrow, tinman and lion. Off to see the wizard.

Angie, the brain. General and nurse. David loves her, but not as much as he needs her. His mirror, his spotlight, his battery, his shield, his darer of dreams and his spine when he has none. She is steel when he wants her to be steel and sugar when he wants her to be sugar. He never has to tell her which. The beauty of Angie is that she always knows.

Mick, the heart. Gilder and maestro. Quiet as drizzle with a headful of thunder. However great David's art, one touch of Mick's fingers and it becomes only greater. Just listen to what he did to 'All The Young Dudes' – it's his song but *that riff?* – or his back-of-napkin string parts for 'Life On Mars?', 'Five Years' and 'Rock 'N' Roll Suicide'. And, just like Angie, David never has to ask. Mick is his musical sixth sense made flesh.

Tony, the courage. Granter of wishes. Defries freed David from his old manager, Ken Pitt, and his old record label, just as he said he would. He found him a better deal, just as he said he would. And now they're breaking away from Gem, just as he said they would. Laurence, ever reasonable, has agreed to a settlement. David doesn't need to know the particulars of terms and percentages, only that they're free, him and Tony, together, to set up a new company on their own. *Their* company. Whatever Tony says, Tony makes happen. Like he made this happen. The flights, the hotel, the limo, New York, Elvis Presley. All courtesy of RCA Records & Tapes. Just as the good book of the Colonel decrees: *'Let someone else pick up the expensive overhead.'*

The Colonel. He'll be waiting for them at the end of their journey. As signatories to the same label, they've been promised a private conference, manager to manager and star to star. Tempting fate, Defries had Dai leak a story to last week's *NME*.

'Bowie meets Presley: David planning to catch Elvis's show at New York Madison Square Garden and "meet the King" at a post-show reception.'

Defries is more interested in meeting the Kingmaker. The real hero of Hopkins's book: the ex-carnie who boasts about making chickens 'dance' by putting them in cages with electric hotplates covered in straw; the con artist who sold hotdogs that were mostly bun and onions, kidding the dupes who bought them that the sausage he'd already placed in the dirt was the one they must've dropped by mistake; the odds-beater who demanded $1 million a Hollywood picture for a Memphis truck driver who can't even act, and got it. A man after his own double-or-quits gall.

The limo jerks, swerving jaywalkers as it dives down Midtown. Yellow cabs, blue neon, red bars, green delis, black chicks, white cops, grey vendors selling the last of today's *Times* with its front-page photo of a naked nine-year-old Vietnamese girl in napalm agony, *Grease* at the Broadhurst – *'it's the dancingest show in town!'* – and, count them, one, two, three, four, five cinemas showing *The Godfather*. David feels the energy of the city banging on the windows like a drunken friend. Defries takes another look at his wrist.

So does Rocco Laginestra. The thin, dark-haired Italian-American churchgoer and President of RCA Records sits eight rows from the front of the stage in Madison Square Garden. His watch says it's almost 9.25 p.m. The King will be out soon and you can chew the expectation in the air like candyfloss. Rocco is surrounded on all sides by fellow industry executives, loose-collared and martini-eyed, apart from the four empty seats directly to the left of him. He looks up the aisle. He looks at the stage. He looks back at his watch.

Where the fuck are they?

They are gridlocked when the lights dim, the drums rumble, the horns parp and the band and orchestra strike up Strauss's theme from *2001: A Space Odyssey*. They are jumping reds when a man in a sparkly caped white suit enters stage left to a zillion bolts of lightning from Instamatic cameras. They are crawling towards the Garden's giant concrete doughnut ringed by souvenir touts waving pictures of Elvis's face when he starts to sing 'That's All Right'. They are wobbling out of the limo and fixing their hair and clothes when it finishes and he mumbles 'Thangoo, goodevenin'' to a hurricane of applause. They are being guided through the lobby as the band kick in to 'Proud Mary'. They are being led by an usher to their row as a doped kingly eye is distracted by a shock of red hair bobbing up the aisle. So is Rocco's. He waves them towards him with a daft grin of relief.

They are here.

Here, 3,000 miles from a Middlesbrough now obliterated from memory. Angie 'OH MY GOD!'s for all of them, her voice lost in the screaming buzz of 20,000 other oh-my-godding New Yorkers. This is real life, and that, up there, is Elvis Presley. Elvis outside a television set, not on a cinema screen: here, wiggling his microphone, jiggling his leg and hula-hooping his hips, fluorescent white and firework gold and crystal sparkles, as starry as a superstar could ever be. David can't take his eyes off his clothes. Angie's undress his body. Mick's jump back and forth following the hands of guitarist James Burton. Defries's bounce around the arena like a loose pool ball in a fit of mental arithmetic: fans times number of seats, times average ticket cost, plus souvenir concessions. He can smell the Colonel like one of his sucker hotdogs. He just can't see him.

He won't. Later, there'll be cufflinked handshakes and company drinks and American hellos and English thank-yous and giggling questions about David's clothes and embarrassed laughs when Defries is mistaken for Tom Jones. But Elvis and his keeper will have long left the building.

Tonight, David will sleep heavy and deep in pedestal dreams of white capes and glory glory hallelujah. Tomorrow, he'll have already forgotten that whatever Tony says doesn't always happen.

EVERYTHING CHANGES. In a long weekend, in a stamp on a passport and a Heathrow landing. David, gone only three days, returns to a new land with a new language. Without trying to, he invented it. Him and Marc together – both their photos, side by side, on the cover of the *NME*'s pull-out *What's On* national gig guide and a two-word headline.

'GLAM ROCK'

It is christened. Less as a description, more as a politer euphemism. For months, the pop press have struggled to define the new rock'n'roll made by men who don't dress like the average Double Diamond drinker. The Davids, Marcs and Alices on intimate terms with a mascara spoolie. And if they're less than real men, then their music must be less than real music. Not proper rock, but 'fag rock'. 'An unwieldy title at the best of times,' dismisses David, who knows it won't stick even before the subeditors. Until they replace harsh 'fag' with subtle 'glam' and the emphasis shifts from the sexual to the sartorial. From now on it's the trousers that matter, not where the wearer pokes the contents.

The week glam is named glam is the first to see a record by Gary Glitter enter the Top 40 and the last T. Rex will ever spend at number 1. A week when Malcolm McDowell's droogie bowler and false eyelashes find a rival in Liza Minnelli's as *Cabaret* sashays into the West End snapping suspenders, swastikas and bold bisexuality. Its poster tag line: 'Divine decadence.' Glam finds an immediate kindred celluloid spirit. Weimar sleaze high-kicks into the sparkly '72 street wardrobe beside saucy flapper, clogged smoothie and rock'n'roll cutie-pie. The hour has come. The stage is all set.

The stage is a television studio in Manchester. David is here with his band to record a performance of 'Starman' for a children's show co-hosted by two glove puppets. *Lift Off with Ayshea* is the decompression chamber between *Play School* and *Top of the Pops*, presented by the same pretty Ayshea wearing the same 'A' pendant necklace she also wears as a communications officer defending Earth from extraterrestrials in *UFO*. If glam rock has a nursery, then Ayshea's *Lift Off* is it. The Sweet were on it last week and Slade will be on it next. Between them, David appeals to the same 5 o'clock minds whose eyes are first to witness him in full flame-haired colour singing 'Starman' in Freddie's new gold, blue and red jumpsuit as giant glitter stars twinkle behind him on a spaceblack backdrop. The programme will air next Wednesday on ITV against Mr Jinks and Pixie and Dixie over on BBC One. The kids who catch it might as well be watching an episode of *UFO*. Singer and subject merge as one, and before mums cry 'Tea's ready!' pocket money priorities shift.

Tonight, a Thursday, David arrives back home in Beckenham long before the streetlamps blink to life the other side of 9 p.m.

Tomorrow, Friday, will be another warm midsummer's day of daisy chains, Lyons Maid and radios whispering *'starry, starry, night'*. A day when shop assistants at Virgin Records on Oxford Street slap £1.95 price stickers on their first shipment of *The Rise And Fall Of Ziggy Stardust And The Spiders From Mars*.

Seven months after he started it, five since its cover photo was taken, four since he finished it, the fifth album by David Bowie lands on the last stroke of glam's baptism like a splash of holy water.

The sound of *The Rise And Fall Of Ziggy Stardust And The Spiders From Mars* is the sound of everything glam has been throughout its nameless 18-month infancy, and still is in this week's singles chart. Marc's 'Metal Guru', Elton's 'Rocket Man', Slade's 'Take Me Bak 'Ome'. You could cut tiny squares out of each of these and place them next to 'Starman', 'Lady Stardust' and 'Suffragette City' and be fooled into thinking they're from the same silvery cloth. David's album does not change glam's established colour spectrum. The reds are still crunchy electric glam reds.

The violets are still romantic orchestral glam violets. What it changes is their luminosity.

The Rise And Fall Of Ziggy Stardust And The Spiders From Mars is first heard in long hours of natural starlight. Made in wintertime, it becomes a sticky summer album in the sticky summer of *Exile On Main Street*, *American Pie* and *Slade Alive!* It spins on the same turntables, on nightless days of blue skies turning very slightly indigo, with windows and curtains open wide, its freckled owners lost in the lonely mystery of its hand-tinted sleeve and the inner bag proofread by David's soundman, Robin, who took it upon himself to correct the lyrics as he thought he'd heard them. And so Ziggy's intended Elvis '68 Comeback 'leather messiah' distorts into a mysterious 'leper messiah' and a 'water-wall' calling becomes a 'wall-to-wall' carpet. Nobody listening will ever know any different. Nobody needs to.

Nobody has to make *sense* of David's album. Most of the critics happily surrender, sticking to chucking superlative bouquets with only a handful bothering to spare a mid-paragraph shrug for some *'not well-defined'* sketchy shared theme of *'the destruction of a rock star'* involving this *'vague character'* Ziggy. None of them call it a 'concept album' because no sane human being could possibly find any sequential plot between the subject of 'Moonage Daydream', a song he wrote over a year ago for his short-lived Arnold Corns band, and 'It Ain't Easy', a spiritual whinge written by Ron Davies that was supposed to go on *Hunky Dory* and probably should have instead of spoiling side one of *The Rise And Fall Of Ziggy Stardust And The Spiders From Mars*. David's album is conceptual only as far as The Beatles' *Sgt. Pepper* was conceptual, only as far as being a long-playing record of mostly unconnected songs presented to the public as being by, or about, some dressed-up alter ego of the pop artists who made it as pictured on its cover. With another cover, another title, *The Rise And Fall Of Ziggy Stardust And The Spiders From Mars* would still be 11 songs by David Bowie that could have very easily been 11 different songs, and almost were, and if they had, then the same point being missed by anyone trying to join dots that don't exist between 'Soul Love' and 'Hang On To Yourself' would be missed trying to join dots that don't exist between 'Velvet Goldmine' and 'Holy Holy'. Because the point is not what any one part of it means. The point is what *all* of it means.

The Rise And Fall Of Ziggy Stardust And The Spiders From Mars is 39 minutes of pop music over two sides of vinyl in a cardboard sleeve for the suggested retail price of £2.19. Shop around, at Virgin or One Stop, and you'll find it for just under two quid. That makes it just a little bit more expensive than one month's rental of a black-and-white television set to watch *Pot Black* in all its subtle shades of grey. In June 1972, this is your choice. Colour or black-and-white. Oz or Kansas. Life or death.

The difference between life and death. That is what *The Rise And Fall Of Ziggy Stardust And The Spiders From Mars* means. Not actual mortal death, but the even deathlier living spiritual death which in June 1972 is the sort of life Maggie wants you to live. The one where you do what your parents and teachers tell you, and study hard, and pass your exams, and get a dull but respectable job involving polished shoes and ties and paperclips, then get married to someone of the opposite sex, whether you're that way or not and whether you love them or not. Then take a mortgage on a house that will give you an ulcer where you'll come home each evening to the smell of insecurity and ruined recipes by Robert Carrier, which you'll drown with Benito sherry before slumping on your settee and praying whatever the box has to offer is enough to tranquillise that scream inside your head, like the hideous wild inhuman scream of a medieval prisoner being dragged to the chopping block, which is the first noise rattling your skull when you wake up each morning and the last thing rattling it when you lose consciousness each night. Because it's the same scream you hear in your head all day every day as you call people 'sir', and jam your stapler, and fork your peas, and circle ads in the *Mail* for P&O Ferries, and laugh weakly at *It's a Knockout*, and do whatever it is this rigid quick-set blancmange of an existence you've made for yourself demands just because you genuinely thought, or hoped, or were hoodwinked into believing by the cabal of lying bastards pulling your strings since the day you were born, that all this indigestion and polyester is the absolute limit of what human life has to offer. Because you never knew you had a choice. You never knew there was another life.

The Rise And Fall Of Ziggy Stardust And The Spiders From Mars is the other life. The sort of life David Bowie wants you to live. The life informed by every lesson he's learned from 25 years of Jack Kerouac, Little Richard, Lindsay Kemp, The Velvet Underground, Beckenham Arts Lab, Stanley

Kubrick, the Sombrero club, *Performance* and Marc Bolan. All those roads have taken him here. Frozen in time on Heddon Street beneath the sign for K. West furriers, asking a question of every kid now holding the finished record in their hands.

What do you want?

Their trousers, or mine?

Black-and-white, or colour?

That life, or *this*?

Do you really want to spend the rest of your life in *their* world of commuter trains, lawnmowers, short back and sides, missionary position with the lights out and the constant fear of being found out?

Or *our* world, dancing free to be whoever and whatever you choose? A movie star, a rock'n'roll bitch, a Marilyn, an Elvis, a Nureyev, a Veruschka, a cosmic yob, a spaced-out queen, a prince from another planet, a Byzantine figure in a changeless landscape.

Because now you can. Any and all of them, on any filthy half-lit shit-strewn backstreet, in any cig-stinking phone box, in any playground, in any bedroom, in any town. Because now you know. Because if the cover hasn't already told you, the music will.

You are not alone. And you're wonderful.

IT IS ALMOST A QUARTER of the way through the decade when *The Rise And Fall Of Ziggy Stardust And The Spiders From Mars* goes on sale on the 898th day of the Seventies.

Everything changes.

TEN

FOUR YEARS AGO, before David Bowie was ever Ziggy Stardust, when T. Rex were still trippy Tyrannosaurus Rex and their lambish singer not yet a pop star, *Melody Maker* asked Marc if he ever worried how success might affect him.

'I can't really get hung up on a pop ego thing,' said Marc, not taking the question very seriously. 'If I get a hit, I'll change my name to Zinc Alloy and wear an aluminium suit.'

That was July 1968.

In June 1972, on the day *The Rise And Fall Of Ziggy Stardust And The Spiders From Mars* is released, the man who never did change his name to Zinc Alloy, despite half a dozen Top 10 hits including four number 1s, is in Manchester having his curls sandblasted by 5,000 screaming kids. Most of them screaming his name. The rest screaming because they've just collapsed under the weight of thousands of other kids surging towards the stage in a teenage tsunami. Jaws break and lungs flatten but nobody quite dies so Marc, in his aluminium-looking suit, and T. Rex chug on, as planned, until the last fuzzy whang when he unstraps his Les Paul, smiles, waves, then turns and flies at insect speed straight through backstage, down to the goods bay, up the steps and onto the revving coach as his stage amp hums with the dying hope of an encore that never comes. The kids keep screaming. The coach vanishes into the distance. The house lights go up. The body count begins.

Two hundred miles and a hazy conversation with a travelling *NME* reporter later, Marc returns to his flat in Maida Vale where he and Mickey posed on the balcony for the photo on the cover of this week's *Jackie*, as if the potential vigil of readers already manically graffitiing his doorstep needed any more clues to his whereabouts. His curtains are drawn and will stay drawn. He is tired and fluey and drunk, with a headful of powders, some of them Beecham's, some of them Chelita's. He sloshes Cognac into a glass and adds it to the bottle already burning his stomach, slumps on his Chesterfield, one satin leg aloft, knee crushing the folds of his blue elephant coat, and squints at his stack of records. Face-front is an Elvis Presley bootleg. He stares solidly at the cover, reading the title and gulping his brandy. His heart wants to laugh but his brain wants to cry. It's called *I Wanna Be A Rock'n'Roll Star*.

This is what success has done to Marc Bolan.

'I live in a goldfish bowl,' he'd said last night on the bus. 'I've become a recluse. Apart from the gigs I haven't been out of the house for two weeks.'

In his bowl, the goldfish sleeps through the morning. His wife, June, shakes some food out in Boink's cage, plops a bag in a mug, boils the kettle and risks the thinnest twitch of the curtains. At least a dozen of them down there already. It's Saturday. By afternoon there'll be three times as many, probably more. They're getting noisier, bolder and cheekier, stealing his bin bags, chipping off bits of brick and wood and even felt-tipping love hearts with 'DAVID' instead of 'MARC'. They don't mean Bowie. They mean Cassidy. 'Keith Partridge' off the telly: the Californian sap-magnet who all the girls' mags have gone daffy about, and who *almost* knocked 'Metal Guru' off number 1 with his fix of pure puberty heroin, 'Could It Be Forever'. Marc is *'raw and meaty'* to Cassidy's *'neat and dreamy'* says *Mirabelle*, who happily agitate the partisan battle lines one pin-up at a time. Those enemy hearts by Marc's gate aren't vandalism: they're acts of pop terrorism.

June knows they have no choice but to find a new home, and soon. Marc wakes, rubbing his brandy-pickled eyes and sniffs something about being too busy to think about it. The new T. Rex album, *The Slider*, is imminent. He's still finishing his film, not the science-fiction one about his 'cosmic messiah' which he reminded Radio Luxembourg about last month in a blaze of pants on fire, but a real one, based around T. Rex's Wembley gig, directed by his new boogaloo chum Ringo, who also stars in it alongside Elton, a stuffed zebra and the man who plays Catweazle. And then there's all this injunction hassle against his old manager who's trying to release an album of 20 of his old demos without his consent. This coming week, Marc's lawyer will be sending out the writ. As the named plaintiff, as required, the paperwork will bear his home address.

In the public interests of legal reportage, the *Evening Standard* print it.

'*Marc, who lives in Clarendon Gardens, Maida Vale . . .*'

THE *EVENING* FUCKING *STANDARD*!

Now *every* kid in the city knows *exactly* where he lives. So does every kid of every commuter who doesn't leave their crumpled copy on the train home to suburban Monotonyshire. Tomorrow half the playgrounds in England will know. One short street with 34 houses not even five minutes' walk from the Bakerloo line. Trebor couldn't have done more damage if they'd stuck his address on packets of Refreshers and lobbed them over school gates.

Marc reads it and freaks. June shrieks. Boink squeaks. Bootleg Elvis laughs.

The fans gasp and sink to their knees. But not over the *Standard*.

It's another story in the same day's *Mirror*, picking up on the new *NME* that went on sale in the capital late yesterday. A conversation Marc mistily remembers in the back of the tour bus after the violence of Manchester, about his gigs becoming too dangerous and not wanting to carry on. Just 'one more tour' and 'that will be the last'. It might have been the Beecham's talking, but just like all the stuff about giraffes growing out of his head and being friends with Fellini, it came out of his mouth all the same. Because there it is, on the cover, in letters as bold and black as the felt-tipped 'DAVID's on his perimeter wall and the pit of fresh hell ripping open his soul.

'BOLAN TO QUIT?'

YOU COULD EASILY fit all the fans that turn up in Clarendon Gardens over the weekend in the upstairs ballroom of the Croydon Greyhound. But you'd struggle to squeeze them in its downstairs function room.

Sunday night and the hothouse is packed with the couple of hundred bodies it takes to start turning people away at the door. Those who've made it inside aren't the sort you'd meet in Clarendon Gardens reeking of cheesy puffs and Femfresh. They're older, stubblier, with hoppy breath and tarry fingers that have possibly never touched a page of *Jackie*. More the kind who read the *Maker*. One of them even works for them.

Some of the crowd recognise him. He's that moustached bloke from *The Old Grey Whistle Test*, Richard Williams. He was on it again this Tuesday, introducing the band he's come all the way to crumby Croydon to see again tonight, even though they're only the support. Any excuse. The way he feels about this band isn't so different from the way the Maida Vale suffrage mob feel about Marc, even if Richard probably doesn't see it that way. But his column in last week's *Radio Times* speaks for itself.

'Quite simply, Roxy Music are destined to save the world.'

Their loudest apostle, but he's not alone. Richard's inky brethren liken them to the closest thing to a British version of The Velvet Underground and *'the biggest breakthrough since frozen pizza'*. They've been described as simultaneously futuristic and revivalist, experimental and pastiche. They themselves list their influences as Frank Sinatra, Ethel Merman, the Ink Spots, Marcel Duchamp and Andy Warhol. On record they sound more like Acker Bilk and the Daleks. Six months ago they weren't even signed, but now they've just released their self-titled debut which the *NME* nominate *'the best first'* they can remember. John Peel agrees. *'It is magnificent.'* Maybe Roxy Music really *are* destined to save the world?

Tonight, all they need to save is the attention of a packed pub in Croydon. They don't have to try hard, dressed as they are like the inside of a snazzy boutique on Kensington High Street. Specifically, Che Guevara, the shop of their friend Antony Price, the 'bummy' pedal pushers designer who styles the band in a rainbow of lamé, animal print and varying altitudes of stackheel. Roxy are inarguably 'glam' but in sound only arguably 'rock'. This is why chin-pinchers like Richard like them. They're not teenybop, more further-education-bop. The songs are very clever, played by people who know it, particularly the one with kiss-me lips, Quant-crayoned eyelids and the last hurrah of a blond scalp who calls himself simply 'Eno', jerking the controls of his synthesizer with the erratic impatience of a JCB driver, often making similar noises.

The five others include: a saxophonist with a Ming the Merciless collar, Andy, who also blows oboe; a guitarist, Phil, who looks like a bluebottle playing a Stratocaster; and the singer, Bryan, a sleazy-eyed Space Elvis whose default crooning face is like a society toff sipping an overly acidic cocktail, and whose default croon is the sound of them gargling it. This is no mean expressive feat when you're singing about car number plates. In chorus or cloth you really couldn't make Roxy up. Credit where it's due, this haughty bunch actually have.

Croydon gives its credit with old-fashioned applause. The Greyhound isn't so big that David doesn't hear it in his dressing room. Roxy are his invited support. He's never met them before, but he likes their album which came out the same day as his own last Friday. He's just read Richard's lathering review of it in this week's *Maker*, slightly galled since they still haven't got round to reviewing *Ziggy* yet. At least they redeemed themselves with their latest Lou Reed interview. He called David 'the only interesting person around', adding how 'everything has been tedious, rock'n'roll has been tedious, apart from what David's doing'. Lou knows it. In another hour, so will Croydon.

David and his Spiders have played forty gigs since Aylesbury. Forty gigs tighter. Forty gigs braver. Forty gigs flashier. Gears have shifted, muscles strengthened, mistakes corrected and showstoppers finessed. There are new clothes, including a caped white satin suit he asked Freddie to make him, inspired by the one he saw on Elvis. Shocking new moves, with Mick – forty gigs more sequined, more blond, more glam, more game – allowing David to grab his arse with both hands as he sinks down to his knees and simulates a blow job by gnawing his guitar strings. And there are new faces behind the stage poking between the gaps in the amps. Hull faces, with Hull voices to multiply the backstage chorus of roll-up-licking flattened vowels already trodden by Mick, Trevor and Woody. Old friends from a Yorkshire B-roads past of cold Transit vans and colder village halls. One is Pete, tall and white with a heavy jaw, whose job is looking after the stage equipment. The other is Stuey, chunky and black with a light hobble, whose job is looking out for David. Back in Hull, Stuey was a pub bouncer. There are things he has done to drunken sailors er'ly in the morning that don't bear singing about. Now all he has to do is keep teenage fingers from tearing David's trousers; if he has to break a few in the process, then that's just the job as he's been paid to do it. The fiercest thing about Stuey is his loyalty.

David is going to need him. He can feel it on his skin, an acceleration, an exhilaration, like everything is getting faster and sharper. These past two weeks it's unmistakeable in the faces of the front rows, the intensified glossy-eyed hunger of zealous disciples with beglittered cheeks and spiked fringes, the same spreading shadows who loiter patiently by the stage door clutching fresh copies of *Ziggy* in the hope he'll bless theirs with his signature. After ten days on sale it's broken the Top 20. The *Maker* will celebrate it, and themselves, by putting him on the cover again next week.

'The man most likely to has done it again, as we front-paged him back in January.'

This has never happened to David before. Bodyguards, Top 20 albums, front pages. It is everything Angie has been telling him he deserves and everything Defries has promised him will occur. For the last month he's been billboarding David with full-page press ads, every week, for both the album and his June tour. One sell-out of the poky Croydon Greyhound won't justify that expense, but the legend is priceless. The small crowd who couldn't get in tonight will become 'over 1,000 disappointed fans' by the time Dai's finished his press release tomorrow. Every paper will print it without challenge. Hype becomes fact. Fact becomes demand. Demand becomes power. The Colonel's basic logic of how to make a superstar. Everything is going exactly to plan.

'Nothing is ever going to be the same again.'

David says it out loud. Not smiling, not frowning, not scared, not ecstatic, just accepting. The calmness of a man walking a tightrope over Niagara Falls who has just passed the point of no return. There is the violent roar of the churning abyss below and there is a thin line stretching forward to whatever journey's end lies through the fog of misty spray. But the moment for panic has passed. You know you cannot, must not fall. So you take one step at a time, the wind of destiny on your back, one foot in front of the other. Alone, among the clouds and out of reach. Until fate's gravity brings you down again. To Croydon.

Richard watches, unimpressed. Tomorrow he'll tell everyone in the *Maker* office that Roxy were marvellous, as ever, but he really doesn't see what all this Bowie fuss is about, even as his boss, Ray, signs off that week's issue with David on the front. They'll also be running Michael's overdue review of *Ziggy* which chucks another garland round his neck. David will be so touched by their support he'll conspire with Defries to place another full-page advert in the following week's *Maker*: a photograph of him fellating Mick's guitar on stage inscribed with a hand Tipp-Exed message: 'Thanx to all OUR people for making ZIGGY. I love you, Bowie x.'

The savage waters rumble. The tightrope tautens. One step at a time.

ELEVEN

WHAT HAPPENED WAS THIS. Me and Brenda both sent off for tickets but I was the one what got them and as soon as I opened the letter I screamed and went running straight round the corner to hers. I said Brend! Brend! You'll never guess! And she said what? And I said we're only going to Top of the Pops ain't we! And you should've seen the look on her face! Then she screamed and we both screamed and her brother Gordon told us to shut up but we didn't care cos we was going to Top of the Pops.

I was a bit worried mum wouldn't let us go cos it was a Wednesday and she said what about school the next day. But I said it wouldn't be late and then I fibbed and said Brenda's mum would drive us back after work which wasn't true as she was on nights but mum said all right and then I prayed that she wouldn't go round and ask and she never did and THANK GOD! But then I remembered that thing in the papers about that girl what killed herself cos her mum wouldn't let her go to Top of the Pops and Brenda said that maybe mum was scared to stop me in case I did the same. And maybe she's right. I don't know why that girl did that. Brenda says she must've been a nutjob. I wouldn't kill myself just cos I got stopped from going to Top of the Pops unless I found out afterwards David Cassidy was on and I missed him in which case then I might. Me and Brenda are nutjobs about Dreamy David Cassidy. All we talked about the week before Top of the Pops was what if he's on it and what we'd do and what we'd say to him and we made up all these stories and Brenda was being right daft and making me die laughing like she always does.

We was so excited when Wednesday came and school was even worse than normal and it was double geography with Farts and me and Brenda was just BORED BORED BORED! And we kept whispering about Top of the Pops and Dreamy David and Farts threw his duster at us and yelled at us to be quiet and I thought oh my god what if he gives us detention! But he didn't. Then the bell went and we ran home to Brenda's to get changed. I picked my rainbow V-neck with my black suede skirt and my new plum tights. Brenda picked green hotpants with boots and her tight yellow top cos it shows her boobs off cos she's bigger than me. We both had the new beads we got from Woolies last weekend. Brenda put hers in a knot so it dangled down her front. I just looped mine. We did our eyes cloud blue and wore plenty of Lip Shock and Brenda said there was no way anyone would know we was 14. Anyway we had a plan that if anyone asked to say we was 16. That ain't that big a fib cos I'm gonna be 15 in a few weeks. I'm a Leo. Dreamy David is an Aries and the horoscopes said that Aries and Leo are a perfect match. Brenda is a Libra like Marc Bolan.

Brenda's mum was at work so it was just us and Gordon. He was being a pig to us and playing his music dead loud. I'd told mum I'd have tea at Brenda's but we didn't bother cos we was too excited and we wanted to get going so on the way to the Tube we got some crisps and pop. I got a bag of chicken fry and Brenda got cheese and onion and we both got Pepsis but we was too excited to eat much. We sat together on the train and we was laughing at our reflections in the window and making faces and just being daft like we always is. This man was giving us looks and we didn't care and just laughed even more. We was laughing that much we nearly forgot to get off at White City. Brenda asked the ticket man where the BBC was and he said just out there on your left. That's when we really started getting nervous in a good way and we both had some gum to calm down a bit. Brenda said it would help make us look older too.

As we got near we was looking out just in case we saw any of the stars going in but we didn't. Brenda said she saw Bruce Forsyth but I don't think it really was him. There was a man by the main gate and we told him we was gonna see Top of the Pops. He looked us up and down a bit funny and Brenda was chewing her gum and saying we got tickets mister! Then he pointed us down another bit and then we got there and there was already tons of people queuing up outside. There was two big girls in front of us and Brenda asked them if they'd heard if

David Cassidy was gonna be on and one of them said they hadn't and pulled a face and sort of laughed and not in a nice way. She was a right snotty cow now I think about it. There was a boy in front of them who heard us and he looked round the snotty cows and smiled at us and said wotcha! Brenda said wotcha! back and then looked at me all naughty and chewed her hair and looked right back at him. The boy had black hair and a red shirt under a stripey tank top and I definitely didn't fancy him. Later Brenda said she didn't fancy him either even though she was being all giggly but she said she was just chatting him up for a laugh. She does that a lot! He asked us where we was from so we told him and then he asked us if we liked Slade. We said they was OK. He said he liked Slade and then he started going on about them being on it last week and how good they was and how he hoped they was on it this week too. Brenda said later he must be dead thick cos they was only on it last week cos they was number 1 and now they ain't so why would Top of the Pops have them back. And she was right cos they wasn't cos Donny Osmond's number 1. But he kept going on and on about Slade and he was right annoying and I started to wish that she'd never said wotcha back at him but then suddenly the crowd started moving cos they was letting us go inside and we didn't talk to him again.

I had our tickets ready and there was a man at a desk where you had to show them. My heart was beating cos I thought they was gonna ask how old we was but they never did. They told us where to go and then we just followed the others down this corridor which was a bit like school or a hospital with a shiny floor and swing doors and that. Then there was a room where people could leave their bags and stuff and toilets so we went in and had a squirt of Dri-Mist and put on some more Lip Shock. There was tons of other girls in there with the same idea sorting themselves in the mirror and you could tell everyone was excited cos they was giggling and talking about who was gonna be on and someone said Donny Osmond and Brenda poked her tongue out in the mirror at me and we both laughed.

Me and Brenda have talked about Donny and we both think he's dishy but he's too young even though he's 14 like us and anyway he's nowhere near as dishy as Dreamy David or as good a singer. It makes me dead mad cos David should have been number 1 cos Could It Be Forever is the most smashing song anyone has ever done and I don't understand why it wasn't. Me and Brenda like Marc Bolan too but Could It Be Forever is tons and tons of times better than Metal Guru and anyway that song doesn't make any ruddy sense! Brenda still likes Marc and so do

I but she likes him more. Like when Rachel Hunter said that Marc was dying of leukaemia Brenda got really mad. She's another nutjob! Rachel Hunter I mean. She said she'd been to Marc's house and he asked her in and they had tea and he played her some songs and that he still rings her up now and then to see how she is. She don't half come up with some whoppers! Brenda told her to sod off in the end but I think that's really cos she's still upset that she never got to see him at Wembley and Rachel Hunter did.

Anyway I think Brenda's over it and that's why we're both so mad about David. If he lived in London we know we'd be outside his house all the time but he lives in America. Brenda asked her mum if they could go on holiday to America but she said it was too expensive so they're going to Clacton instead. The next time Dreamy David comes over me and Brenda have already decided we're gonna go to his hotel. Last time he came he stayed in the Dorchester and I know that cos it said it in Fabulous 208 and Brenda says she knows where that is and we think he'll probably go there again cos it's dead posh. We also know when he was there he had to sneak out in a car with a blanket over his head so we'll be clever and watch out for any cars with someone with a blanket on their head. I don't know what we'll do if we see one. I told Brenda I'd throw myself in front of it and make it stop and she said what if it ran over me? But I said maybe David would feel terrible about it and come and see me in hospital. Brenda laughed and said what if I was dead? Then we both laughed and I said well as long as she sorted my grave so it said killed by David Cassidy and then our names would be together forever and he'd have to come and put roses on it every year on the anniversary and that he'd probably write a song about me to say how sorry he was. Brenda calls me bloody cuckoo! I am bloody cuckoo when it comes to David! I KNOW I AM! But it ain't just me. There was that girl what wrote to Mirabelle who was scared she was gonna get the sack cos her boss went out shopping and left her alone and all that time her boss was gone she was on the phone ringing up America trying to speak to David's manager and she knows that when her boss gets the phone bill she'll kill her. I felt sorry for her cos I know just how she feels cos that's the sort of thing I would do if I got a job. Me and Brenda tried to go into Mirabelle the other week cos there's a woman there called Linda and she MET DAVID! And she made a tape of him talking and it said they'd had fans coming into their office to listen to it so we thought we'd go too so we got the train and found the building but it was Saturday and it was shut. Then we was gonna bunk off and go again but then they said they'd had

77

to stop letting fans listening to it cos the tape was wearing out so we never did get to hear it. But I've wrote to that Linda and I've asked her tons of things about what David is like but she ain't written back yet. Mirabelle is the best magazine cos David writes a column for it. He also writes one for Fabulous 208 but I think the Mirabelle one's better. I think that's cos he gets tired writing two every week which is why one ain't as good even though I still read both. Mirabelle also got us to tell the BBC to put The Partridge Family back on telly cos they had it on then they took it off so Mirabelle made this coupon and told us to fill it in and send it back to them and then they was gonna show the coupons to the BBC and make them stick it on again. THEY'D BETTER! I sent my coupon and Brenda sent hers. Brenda likes Mirabelle best too but sometimes we both have to get Jackie as well for the posters.

When we came out of the toilets they took us through into the studio and you won't believe this but it felt really small. It was like a big black box and it went up high with lights and bits of metal and things all above but the main bit we was in was just like a square and there was only a couple of stages and though they looked like the ones on Top of the Pops we still couldn't believe this really was Top of the Pops. They had these cameras what was massive which they wheeled all over the place like giant shopping trolleys but they was big as phone boxes and there was tellies above your head which showed what the cameras was looking at and then Brenda said LOOK! and waved and we looked and it was us up on the telly!

There must've been about 40 of us or something. Not as much as it looks on telly. They had this man who was pointing and telling us where we all had to stand and it was a bit like being in PE being told oi! don't go there! go there! and we didn't like him cos he was dead grumpy. But then they played some music and it wasn't Top of the Pops yet but they was getting us in the mood and everybody started dancing so me and Brenda did too. And then guess who came in? TONY BLACKBURN! He was quite dishy but I think Brenda was disappointed cos she wanted it to be Stewpot. It was dead funny seeing him in real life and he was waving and saying hi to people and we waved at him and then the next thing it was all starting proper and they played the Top of the Pops music and then we all had to dance to this other record. Me and Brenda was just too busy giggling at everything cos it wasn't like it was real and we kept looking at each other thinking is we really on Top of the Pops? We was so excited that we didn't realise that what they was doing was picking people out to dance nearest the stage so they'd be on telly and by the time we did they'd finished picking and they never picked us. But it was only Lulu so we didn't mind. We didn't know her song but it was OK and we wasn't really watching her as we was hoping that the man would see us and pick us out for the next one. Then Lulu was off and they showed this film on the tellies of this rock band called Silver Machine or something and while that was on they was telling everyone to move again to another stage and this time we really tried to get close but we couldn't cos there was already too many dancers on the stage. And guess who was up there? Slade boy! We was so mad cos he was the most rubbishest dancer and all.

BUT OH MY GOD! I nearly forgot. Before that I NEARLY FAINTED didn't I! Cos they said who was coming on and for a moment I thought they said David Cassidy! But it wasn't it was David someone else. He was dead trendy and me and Brenda realised when we seen him that we'd watched him on Ayshea a few weeks ago. He had red hair and big red boots and this shiny costume which was all like a magic carpet and his band was all in gold and silver and that. Sort of a bit like Marc Bolan. But we couldn't see him properly cos we was trying to squeeze in round so the cameras could see us but we couldn't get past these other kids and we was dead annoyed.

Then we all had to move again and that was when me and Brenda thought we might get thrown out cos next it was the willy song by The Sweet! It was Brenda who started it cos the first time we heard it whenever that was she did this thing where she goes little willy willy and then she . . . I can't tell you what she does cos you'd have to see but it is the funniest rudest thing in the whole world and we laugh our knickers off. So there we was at Top of the Pops and there's The Sweet in front of us singing the willy song. And she's gone red and I've gone red and we're pretending to dance but she gets redder and redder and she's shaking and we're both laughing and I was thinking I was gonna wet myself and we was gonna get sent out for laughing just like at school! But we didn't.

Then we sort of calmed down and just enjoyed the rest of it cos it was all going by so fast. We saw Pan's People and they was amazing dancers and dead pretty and dead nice cos afterwards they looked over and smiled. Then there was the New Seekers who was pretty boring and afterwards Brenda said she couldn't understand why Stewpot asked the singer to marry him as she weren't nothing special. Then there was that Gary Glitter who dressed all glittery like what you'd expect. We was laughing cos he had a horrible hairy chest and Brenda said he looked like a mad gorilla. But we really liked his hey! hey! song cos it was so great for dancing and me and Brenda was right going for it and so was these other girls and there was a whole bunch of us all bopping in a big row and the cameras was looking at us and even Gary Glitter was cheering at us and it was ace!

Then guess what? They played Donny Osmond but it was on the telly screens! So he wasn't really there after all. But everyone still danced and so did me and Brenda even though we know he ain't that good and Puppy Love is no way as good as Could It Be Forever. And then it was almost over but they played one last record and you will never guess who it was? DAVID!!! His new one with the Partridge Family. Kiss me all through the night! YES PLEEEASE!!! Even though he wasn't there and it was only the record it was the best bit I think cos me and Brenda did our best dancing and we both had these big grins on our faces and we was pretty sure the cameras got us cos we looked up at the tellies and we both seen ourselves.

We didn't want it to end but it did. Brenda was looking around and said we should wait in case any of the groups or Tony Blackburn came back out and wanted to chat or take us for a drink or something but they never did. Then we was told to go and get our stuff and next thing we was gone and it was darker outside and it was weird like it was all a big dream or something. We got the train back and walked home together and said night night at the corner and she walked down her road and I walked down mine and we kept waving till we couldn't see each other no more like we always do.

The next day at school was rubbish again and we was both tired but it was dead funny as well cos everyone was jealous and asking us questions and it was like we was a bit famous or something. Sue James asked if we got any autographs and we felt a bit bad cos we didn't. Rachel Hunter kept saying nasty things like she didn't believe us like why was you there on a Wednesday when it's live on telly on a Thursday? Brenda called her a stupid cow and they nearly had a fight but the bell went.

After school Brenda came to ours for tea cos her mum was out and she knew if we tried to watch Top of the Pops with Gordon in he'd just spoil it. Mum made us fish fingers and beans. We had to get in front of the telly before dad got in just in case he started watching something else. It was all boring news and then tennis and he came in and sat down when the tennis was still on and I knew then we'd have to watch Top of the Pops with him which I was hoping wouldn't happen cos he always moans and maybe we'd have been better off round Brenda's with Gordon.

But then it started and I had my camera ready so I could take photos of us on the telly. It was funny seeing it again after seeing it for real in the studio. AND WE WAS ON IT!!! There was a couple of bits when you saw the back of my head and when you saw Brenda and one bit in Gary Glitter when you saw us together and I tried to take photos but it was hard trying to watch telly and take pictures at the same time. The funniest bit was the willy song cos dad was going what's all this rubbish? And we was just shaking laughing and he didn't see what was so funny. It was nice to hear David at the end as well but they should've played more of him. And we still didn't like Donny Osmond much. But later me and Brenda was talking about it and we both said that after dancing to Dreamy David the best thing on it was that David Bowie. I wish we'd got a bit closer to see him when we was there cos when he came on the telly Brenda said he looks sexy don't he! And she laughed and I blushed but I know what she means! His clothes looked smashing and he did this pointy thing with his finger and then him and his dishy guitar player with the blond hair sang together and he put his arm round him. That's when dad yelled something about poofters but he always does that. He even said Marc was a poofter and he isn't cos Mirabelle said he's got a wife called June. Brenda was making me laugh too cos when David Bowie was singing we kept seeing Slade boy in his tank top and his rubbish dancing!

Me and Brenda both said we're gonna go to Top of the Pops again so we're both gonna write off for tickets. The next day we was in maths which is the worst so we sat at the back and wrote lists of who we'd like to see if we got on again. We both said Dreamy David but then I felt sick thinking what if he's on it next week and I missed him by a week. Brenda said she wanted to see Marc Bolan just to annoy Rachel Hunter. I said I'd watch David Bowie again and Brenda said she would too and she's gonna get his record. I made Brenda laugh cos I said we should make sure we go back when Slade was on and dance on stage with them just to annoy you-know-who!

That's pretty much all what happened. Only Gordon just gets more horrible cos he heard me and Brenda talking about David Bowie and he says he definitely is a poofter cos he read it in one of his smelly magazines. And I had to buy Jackie again cos they're doing a MASSIVE poster of Dreamy David you've gotta collect over three weeks and it's GORGEOUS! And my telly photos came out rubbish and you couldn't see anything and Brenda was mad and we fell out cos she said it was my fault for having a rubbish camera. And we wasn't talking for a whole day and I hated it but then she got me a Twix to say sorry so I let her have half of it and we're best friends again. She's even said that if it came to it she'd let me go off with David Cassidy instead of her! I nearly cried. But I think she's really only saying that cos she fancies that other David now . . .

TWELVE

HE SAYS HE ONLY GETS DRUNK when he feels empty. Either he's empty all the time or there's a lot of Lou Reed to fill. He was soused when he landed here last week and he's been soused, or as good as, or quickly on his way to being, or slowly coming back from, every day since. 'I don't have much personality or anything,' he drones to whoever's sitting on the other side of his Johnnie Walker. 'All of my gestures are stolen from other people. I've found I have no control over it. When it wants to show up it does, and when it doesn't I just get drunk.' Which he does until his tongue is numb to the alcohol. Then he'll drink some more till the taste comes back. Lou is a tall glass of Jekyll with a chaser of Hyde. Punchbag friends and lovers are always reminding him of the things he hissed two blackouts ago.

'Well, if I was drunk, it must be true.'

Lou is David's idea of a living genius.

The genius, not yet full, is on stage beside David, the stage where he took the Spiders to see the Sugar Plum Fairy arabesque not six months ago. The official reason for being at the Royal Festival Hall is to 'Save the Whale' as the headliner of a Friends of the Earth charity benefit. Unofficially, David's here to save Lou. From obscurity. From himself.

It is the first time Lou's stood and performed on a British stage. David is satined in good guy white. Lou is velveted in bad guy black, in the outfit Angie picked out for him from Granny Takes A Trip: a matching bolero

83

jacket and trousers, the sleeves and legs decorated with stemmed flowers of beads and sequins. His guitar model is a Country Gentleman and he plays it like a city punk, the only way to play 'White Light/White Heat'. David has surrendered the last portion of his own set so he and the Spiders can become a substitute Velvet Underground with Lou as his very special guest. Along with a prickly 'I'm Waiting For The Man' and an uptight 'Sweet Jane' they help wipe the bad memory of the wrong Velvet Underground who came to England last winter hellbent on reputation damage. The crowd are boisterous in their appreciation, but not even Lou can steal this night from David. He closes with 'Suffragette City', which brings the nearby Thames to boil. *'Wham bam!'* and orange photocopies of David shower over the crush of fans at the front like tickertape as simultaneously tiny stars rain upon the heads of those further back under the balcony. Above them shakes a giant homemade banner spelling out a name in foil stickers from W. H. Smith's. David looks up, squinting through the spotlight, then grins. The banner doesn't say 'BOWIE'. It says 'ZIGGY'.

The tightrope sways. One step at a time.

Two days after *Top of the Pops*, three years after 'Space Oddity', David is finally a pop star again. The Royal Festival Hall acts as a timely coronation, and the reviews that follow – whether multiple *'star is born'* clichés or predictions he'll *'become the most important person in pop music on both sides of the Atlantic'* – the spikes of his paper crown. He has an album in the Top 10, a single steadily cruising up the Top 20, and his own fan club started by a girl in Aylesbury called Hilda, who after two months drumming up slow support in maydays to *Sounds* and *Petticoat* now has a letterbox banging like the walls of a Naples knocking shop.

He also has Lou. The genius has come to London to play some warm-up gigs before starting his new album with help from David and Mick who will arrange and produce. Angie has found him a modern terraced house to rent an ace serve from Wimbledon Centre Court and a cabbie's nightmare fare from any place with a late bar. His first proper show is the following Friday in a newly converted cinema near King's Cross. By the time Lou goes on, it's 2 a.m. on Saturday. He wears the same sequined black velvet bolero suit and dark make-up so his eyes look like a panda and his lips like livor mortis. Backing him are 'The Tots', four kids from Yonkers just old enough to have stopped swapping bubblegum cards who came over with his cabin baggage. They're no Spiders From Mars but they still make a better Velvet Underground than the wrong Velvet Underground. Lou twists a hand in the spotlight and his fingernails twinkle with black polish. Some humourless creep blows a piercing wolf whistle. Lou pinpoints them with a stare like a whaler's harpoon. 'Bet you wish you were as pretty.' Then plays 'Sweet Jane'.

Unseen in the shadows, David melts in awe.

The encore is 'Heroin' and a deaf city of needles tugs another tourniquet. It is 3 a.m. There is another prog band due on after Lou, but their name is unpronounceable and their music unrememberable, and the black-eyed phantoms scatter long before the first rays of the disinfectant dawn.

JULY SUNSHINE MAKES THE JET LAG HANG HEAVIER. Eyes that ought to be sleeping in New York wince at a London much too awake. There are nearly 20 pairs of them. This time yesterday they were softening to pre-flight drinks at Kennedy Airport in full Eastern Standard temporal health. Now they're frowning into their first lousy limey coffee in the Inn on the Park in the bends of Greenwich Mean Time. Some have hangovers and some of those hangovers come on a coaster with Lou Reed's blackened face on it. Last night, after they'd landed in Heathrow and been bussed to their fancy hotel where they were generously watered and adequately fed, someone heard that Lou was playing. Even by New York standards it would've been rude not to go and lend their support, as well as being their duty as a delegation of visiting rock hacks. Their heads didn't hit their pillows until 4 a.m. For the bite-sized oblivion they managed to steal it wasn't worth the drop.

Saturday is theirs to kill as they please. Dodge double-deckers over the road to Hyde Park to sniff the hydrangeas or gawp at the changing of the guard at the Palace. Risk cutting in the snaking queues for Tutankhamun or sit and stew round the corner in the Hard Rock Café and kid themselves they never left. Just make sure that, as per detailed instructions, they're back in the lobby by 5 p.m. Because they haven't been flown all this way for all this money just to buy Tower Bridge snow globes.

The money is RCA's. The caper is Defries's and it's a peach: as pretty as the sparrows the Colonel used to paint yellow to sell as canaries. It's also one of the oldest capers in the book. You make the record label fly over a junket of foreign press to meet your artist and see them in concert and justify the grotesque expense of all the wining and dining on the publicity it'll generate back in their home territory. Not cheap, but still cheaper than one week's billboard rental in Times Square. Either way, the objective is the same. Defries wants America. To get it, he needs America to want David. And to want David, he needs the 18 ambassadors of their music press in the lobby by 5 p.m. to catch that coach.

IT'S NOT THE SAME. How could it be? The last time he was their little secret and you could still buy a ticket on the door. Now he's on *Top of the Pops* and it sells out in under two hours one week in advance. But he's still David – *their* David – and he's still coming back to the same Borough Hall in Aylesbury where it all started. And some of the Friars faithful still manage to sneak in that afternoon and watch him soundcheck, just like old times. And a few of them even scuttle round to go backstage so they can say hello, just like old times. And none of them make it past the solid black Yorkshireman blocking their path like a collapsed mineshaft.

'Over. My. Dead. Body.'

No. It's definitely not the same.

Friars are slow to realise they are merely pawns in Defries's game of transatlantic chess. David is here to perform for them, only so they can perform as besotted maniacs to impress the coachload of Yank cynicism just pulling in to a nearby historic inn for a pre-show roast beef dinner and another torn stub of the RCA chequebook. Their subway map minds try to make sense of where they are. A suburb? A village? An Ealing comedy? Then they get inside Friars and realise they're in some quaint English version of an Elvis Presley movie. There's the star in shiny clothes pulling sexy moves on the stage. There's the smalltown hicks going crazy in the stalls. All very cute. The Americans get the picture long before David rips the top from his skinny body and flings the shreds into the snatching throng.

The coach drops them back in the city just after 1 a.m. Cotton sheets beckon, but someone says the magic word and in a hiccup of reason black cabs are hailed to the scene of last night's crime.

The magic word is 'Iggy'.

Twenty-four hours after Lou rose from the grave, it's The Stooges' chance for a second coming in the same former King's Cross cinema. Iggy found a new jacket in London but he and James never did find a new rhythm section. That's why he's asked Defries to fly his old one over from Michigan to join him – drummer Scott Asheton and his Nazi-loving bassist brother Ron. Theirs is the only blitzkrieg that fits. Like Lou, tonight is Iggy's British live debut. His hair is platinum, his trousers silver, his chest bare. He wears half as much make-up as Lou but with twice the nerve: springing off stage, sitting in fans' laps, groping their flesh and twiddling their hair as he howls about hunger and sickness and tight trousers and chicks in fur boots while the band fuzz and thump at torturous volume. There's a name for this sort of music but the Seventies hasn't had long enough to think about it yet. Regardless of whatever hour of the morning he finishes, Iggy will always be five years ahead of his time.

His flagging countrymen have since lost all track of theirs. Night peels back at the corners in patches of morning purple. There are taxis, elevators and fumbled door keys, and the dreamless sleep that falls like a guillotine.

SUNDAY IS A COLD SPLASH of pain and prairie oysters then the slow gathering of wits and notebooks and batteries and cassettes. No buses today, just a 300-yard slouch up Park Lane to the Dorchester. Doors held open by top hats and gold buttons. A foyer like being First Class on the SS *Titanic* where the smell of money is strong enough for its own insurance policy. Then through the maze of marble and gold to a parkside suite with pink fleur-de-lis wallpaper, matching curtains and crystal chandeliers. The sultan will see you now.

David waits in polka-dotted white, soft as silk pyjamas, bony chest exposed, one cigarette quickly replacing the next. One by one the journalists take their turn to slide into the empty space on the davenport beside him. The faces change but the same questions linger in the air longer than his smoke. They all want to know about his sexuality: he refuses 'to be tied down'. They all want to know if he's 'genuine' or just an image: he says he wants to be 'a prop for my songs'. They all want to know what this Ziggy Stardust thing is really all about.

'Ziggy is a conglomerate rock star,' David starts, then stops. 'Please don't ask me to theorise on Ziggy. Having written it down, there are some things in it that are so personal that I find the whole thing has become a monster . . . there are some things I never dreamed that I would have put in.'

He lights another cigarette and they ask another question. His ears listen but his brain disconnects. Pink. All David sees is pink. Not just the walls and the chairs but the air itself. The world turns pink and everything in it.

Across the room there's Angie, with her own shorter, spikier Ziggy cut, yelling shocking pink speech bubbles as she playfully sinks her teeth into the right tit of the woman from the *Sunday News*. And Lou's here, a mind blacker than his keep-the-fuck-out sunglasses and trousers the colour of tinned salmon. And so is Iggy, in a T. Rex T-shirt so tight it seems sprayed on, beaming his blame-me-for-nuttin' strawberry sundae smile. And David's rosy lips part, and before he knows it out pops a confession of purest fuchsia.

'I definitely like being a star. It's the only thing that I can do that doesn't bore me.'

THIRTEEN

STARMAN SINGER TRAGEDY
"Gay" pop hero killed in holiday car smash

David Bowie – the weirdo pop singer known for his bizarre dress sense – was killed yesterday in a traffic accident in Cyprus.

It is understood Mr Bowie, 25, was driving the car which collided with another vehicle on a level crossing outside the town of Kyrenia. He was pronounced dead at the scene.

Bowie, real name David Jones, is understood to have been holidaying on the island with his wife, Angela, 22, and two of the musicians in his band, Trevor Bolder and Michael Woodmansey. All three were passengers in the same car but survived with minor injuries. No one in the other vehicle was hurt.

His friend and guitar player Michael Ronson told the *Mirror* Bowie had been looking forward to touring the States.

"The last conversation I had with him he was saying how excited he was about going to America," says Ronson who is currently working in Canada. "We all knew he was going to be a superstar over there. I honestly can't believe he's dead. It's just terrible."

Presently at number 10 in the pop charts with his song 'Starman', Bowie first hit the scene in 1969 with 'Space Oddity' about an astronaut whose mission goes badly wrong.

The outrageous singer later made headlines by growing his hair long like a woman and being photographed in dresses. More recently he told a top music magazine he was "gay" and "bisexual" despite being married. He and his wife have a one-year-old son, Zowie, who is believed to be staying with a nanny in London.

A management spokesperson added: "We are much too shocked to make any further comment."

THIS ALMOST HAPPENS. Most of it does. The fortnight in northern Cyprus. A beachside villa with Trevor and Woody and Angie's friends Karl and Shahe. Hot days of purple mountains and a sea so blue it looks squeezed straight from an oil tube. Cool nights of stuffed vine leaves and retsina shivers. Zowie left at home in Haddon Hall with Sue. Mick in Toronto at RCA's behest working on string arrangements for country rock band Pure Prairie League. David at the wheel of a rented car slamming headfirst into another. All that doesn't happen is the dying part.

Instead, nerves shredded but bones intact, David lives to be questioned by Cypriot police who charge him with dangerous driving. He agrees to pay for damages and the case is eventually dismissed. No headlines. No mourning.

No death-shaped spanner sabotaging the schemes of Tony Defries. He leaves Gem's Regent Street office for the last time with the contents of his desk in a cardboard box and one of Laurence's secretaries. He also takes Gem's accountant. Work and home is now the same Chelsea address at the Fulham Road end of Gunter Grove in a converted Victorian meeting hall where men in starched underclothes once lectured on temperance. Defries and his girlfriend Melanie move into the upstairs apartment with a minstrel gallery looking down upon the large office space below. The central feature is a desk long enough to host the Last Supper which is exactly the dimensions Defries requires to accommodate what at first glance appears to be one telephone for every disciple. All of them his. Power is the sound of several lines ringing at once and the sight of a man with a receiver in each hand and a third sandwiched in the folds of his neck. The new company name is the chomped cigar to complete the picture: Mainman.

So far it's only the heading on his stationery. The first calls in and out of Gunter Grove are transatlantic. As a parting gift to Defries, Laurence has agreed to loan him £40,000 to set up another Mainman office in New York where he's been relying on the friends he and David made last year when the cast of Andy Warhol's *Pork* were in town. He's asked actor Tony Zanetta, known as Zee, to find him and Melanie a similar home and office in Manhattan ready for David's American tour, which he's begun putting in place for the autumn with a zeal that would bring a greenbacked tear to the Colonel's granite eye. He's been hustling to try to get David the prized music slot on *The Flip Wilson Show*, America's highest-rating variety show with an audience of over 17 million. He sees David's face on billboards, balloons, T-shirts, button badges, lunchboxes and plastic Ziggy dolls. He smells limousines, penthouses, gold elevators, Hollywood and Madison Square Garden. The sweet aroma of the American dream.

Then the door of Gunter Grove swings open and he smells the American reality of Iggy.

There is no avoiding him. Iggy now lives a five-minute leopard-jacketed saunter round the corner on Seymour Walk with the rest of The Stooges. The good news is that Defries has finally managed to get them into the studio at Olympic in Barnes to start making the album he's promised CBS. The bad news is the tape Iggy's just delivered to his office. Defries presses play and hears grievous bodily harm in 4/4 time. Iggy's words, about giving head and starting fights and being sick, fit the noise like a knuckleduster.

Defries hears enough. He presses the stop button. Iggy grins. A sly 'gotcha' kind of grin. Defries doesn't return it.

'Well?' leers Iggy, tilting his head to one side. 'What do you think?'

Defries thinks David can't come home from Cyprus quick enough.

HE ALMOST DOESN'T. Lightning strikes the wings of his return flight and for the second time in as many weeks David's life flashes before his eyes. The plane judders, mouths scream, stomachs flip and drained faces gibber broken prayers. David turns the colour of a frozen ghost. Before it lands safely he strikes a mental bargain with the Fates never to set foot in another aircraft.

The Fates know his country still needs him. David comes home as the first English summer of glam hits full bloom in spears of purple buddleia rattling in the evening breeze like the sabres of his rivals. First blood goes to Alice Cooper, whose 'School's Out' is the only song you need when you've six weeks without a satchel round your neck watching *The Flashing Blade* with a bowl of Ricicles. The kids send it to number 1 with double thumbs up. Alice has an album of the same name, packaged with the vinyl wrapped in a pair of paper knickers. It outsells Marc's new album, *The Slider*, wrapped in blue quartz riffs and pearly namedrops of Dylan and Pasolini, but otherwise naked. Alice also outsells *Ziggy Stardust*.

This means war.

Roxy Music smell gunfire and switch ammunition to 45 rpm. 'To get on *Top of the Pops* to meet Pan's People,' explains Bryan Ferry. When Andi, Babs, Dee Dee, Ruth and Louise hear the sexy stop-start of 'Virginia Plain' they'll be dragging the band back to the dressing room by their ostrich feathers. Every edge sharp, every surface sparkling, it is a perfect sugar cube of glam. Almost *too* perfect.

If Roxy are the monocled generals on the hilltop, Blackfoot Sue are the muddybooted cannon fodder. 'Standing In The Road' is the best Slade rip-off this side of 'School's Out' and at least they've the noble excuse of being Brummies. Presumably in the interests of physical inclusivity, *Mirabelle* gives them a double-page pin-up, overlooking the fact singer Tom Farmer is as gormless a tater picker who ever slipped on a pair of dungarees. This is especially bad news to their drummer, Dave, who is his identical twin. None of the band are above 5 foot 7. Blackfoot Sue were clearly not made for great heights and number 4 is as giddy a limit as history dare indulge them.

The ground shudders and the bodies fly as the real Slade drop a ten-kiloton rebuke for the folly of trying to sound like Slade. The bloody moral of 'Mama Weer All Crazee Now' is that these things are best left to Slade. 'How on earth can a record like this fail,' asks John Peel, 'and what curmudgeon would want it to?' It can't and it doesn't. Slade say their music's for kids 'to sweat their bollocks off'. As the *Maker* democratically reassures, this doesn't even exclude those born without any: 'ALL THE BAD GIRLS LOVE SLADE!' One week they're being mentioned in the same breath as *A Clockwork Orange*, the next, *Jackie* awards them their own life-story comic strip prettifying their likenesses beyond recognition: Slade really are the droogs you can bring home to meet Mum. In the glam wars of '72, the first Victoria Cross goes to their fringephobic guitarist Dave Hill. *The Sun* calls him 'Sexy Mr Sparkles' because each week he showers an estimated fiver's worth of glitter over audiences while jestering back and forth in the £35 silver high-heel platform boots he has specially made by Todd's in Kensington Market. His cobbler, Lionel, cautions Dave that anything over four inches is too dangerous. 'I tried five and a half,' says Lionel, 'but it looked like a design for a clubfoot.' Dave ignores the warnings and demands an ankle-breaking six: before the first snowflake of Christmas he'll be up to his right knee in plaster of Paris. Just this once, the plastic orange that he always superstitiously carries in his suitcase 'for luck' fails him.

You don't need any magic amulets when you're Mott The Hoople. Last year they were wishing suicide on Tony Blackburn. Now he's playing them at breakfast on Radio 1. Two hours later, so is David 'Diddy' Hamilton, but such is the spell cast by 'All The Young Dudes'. The Rule Britannia of glam takes Mott into the Top 3, making it David's highest charting song to date. Lou is convinced it's 'a gay anthem, a rallying cry to the young dudes to come out in the streets and show that they're beautiful and gay and proud of it'. He joins David at the hip to see them in Guildford, back in the very Civic Hall where it all began four months ago, where Max Wall isn't missed and where the crowd hit the ceiling as David shimmers on stage, a knight in white satin, to join the similarly silver Mott for the encore of 'Dudes'. *'OK, so now they've gone in for the camp bit on stage,'* withers the *NME*, *'but it's subtle poovery.'* Lou mumbles 'told you so' and knocks back another double. As only he knows, glam is a dish best served with shaved legs and a platinum wig. With David's help, Lou's own artillery is now ready to fire.

The days of subtle poovery are numbered.

FOURTEEN

THE PERFECT DAYS OF AUGUST. Long days for David. Mornings looking through the windscreen of his new blue Jaguar as he drives from Beckenham to Soho, Chelsea or Finsbury Park. Afternoons of tense moods and mixing desks, *doo-doo-doos* and cigarettes, band rehearsals and costume fittings, changing schedules and crossings-out. Evenings of Angie and Defries at Mimmo d'Ischia, chilled Pouilly-Fuissé and Spanish waiters, lit dancefloors and glassy-eyed queens, good sex and bad dreams of crashing planes. Long, long days.

'Just givin' it a tune.'

David is watching Lou, who is watching Mick on the other side of the studio gently turn the tuning heads of Lou's Gretsch Country Gentleman. With his shades on it's hard to tell if Lou is actually looking at Mick or just angling his head in a vague general direction. The expression on Lou's mouth suggests he is. The lips don't move but they're twisted as if dying to ask 'what the fuck are you doing to my guitar?' The only reason they don't is because Lou has no idea what Mick just said. *'Jess governor achoo'*? Hull is as foreign a tongue as has ever ricocheted off Lou's cracked sidewalk ears. Sometimes, maybe after the third or fourth repeat, he'll just about grasp what Mick is talking about. Otherwise it's all burbling hobgoblin. Mick carries on tuning, Lou carries on glowering, and David rubs a bent knuckle into his sleepy eye.

'So,' David turns to Lou, 'what is it today?'

Lou's bottom lip juts forward. He makes a low lizardy hum in his throat like a warming engine. It takes several seconds to start.

'"Satellite",' says Lou. The low hum again, this time with the faintest flex of a smile. 'We'll do "Satellite".'

Lou doesn't have to do much. This is his genius, and his curse. Genius, because his songs are like one of Picasso's drawings: a couple of strokes and the picture is complete. No wasted words or sagging chords, everything simple, precise and perfect, and perfect because Lou makes it look simpler than it actually is. Curse, because in making it look so simple he invites the vultures of virtuosity. This is what happened the last time Lou tried to make an album. There was nothing wrong with any of the songs on *Lou Reed*, the solo debut that wobbled out to lukewarm reviews in May. The problem was the producer, Richard Robinson, who saw the beautiful wide negative spaces in Lou's art as sonic ditches begging to be filled with squeals and cymbals and whatever falderals the assembled shooting party of English session musicians, including two members of Yes, cared to toss on top. This is the mistake Lou doesn't want to repeat and the reason he interrupted a meal in Haddon Hall two months ago, just as Angie was dishing out the lemon meringue pie to their guests Anya and Dai, by ringing up to drag David away from the dinner table to ask if he wouldn't mind producing his next album. David spent the rest of the night raving about Lou and playing *Loaded* in a haze of smoke and excitement.

Two months later, only the smoke has cleared. It means more to David than he can put into words. Luckily, he doesn't have to. His job is to put it into music. Lou's music, the way it ought to be heard, embellishing it without blemishing it. A very delicate balance.

That's why he has Mick.

David's is the architect's brain but Mick's is the engineer's. David hears overall shapes; Mick hears supporting structures. With every day he spends in a studio, Mick's harmonic instincts finesse. He arranges music in such a way that it doesn't sound like something added but something revealed, like a secret layer that had always been there, like old wallpaper just waiting for his roll-up-tightening fingers to peel back and expose. It happened here in Trident only a few weeks ago when they were recording

Mott, a song called 'Sea Divers' that Ian thought was a simple piano ballad until Mick's string section began bowing and found something like a tone poem by Sibelius. These are the sorts of things Mick does without blinking, easy as tapping out a tin of Old Holborn.

He does it again with 'Satellite Of Love'. Lou first plays it to David and Mick as a guitar song – that is, played on a guitar as not quite totally tuned as its player is not quite totally drunk, the way Lou's always played it since the dying days of The Velvet Underground. Mick scribbles down the chords, and the turbines in his hardwater Hull brain start sloshing with melodic energy. The guitar becomes a cocktail piano. The middle-eight becomes a recorder solo. The coda becomes a brass fanfare. And those choruses? They sound like bells. Singing bells.

'Bong! Bong! Bong!'

Lou sits in the corner of the control room listening back to the crystal bongs. They're the same three notes Mick used on the opening riff of 'All The Young Dudes'. If Lou notices, he doesn't say, and if he did, he wouldn't care, seeing as he thinks 'Dudes' is the most wonderful single he's ever heard in his life. He thinks what Mick's done to 'Satellite Of Love' is pretty wonderful too. The shades are off and the hooded eyes are soft and misty.

'Ooh! Oh, Daaavid! I *love* that!'

It's Lou's composition painted in Mick's colours but David's is the finishing signature. A cosmic coyote howl bouncing around the planets, out into the endless depths of space.

Space.

The width of a galaxy.

The breadth of an ocean.

The span of a few Soho streets.

The curtains are up in the Palace Theatre where David's friend, Dana, is on stage watching a crucifixion as part of the hottest ticket in town. She's won the coveted role of Mary Magdalene in the West End production of *Jesus Christ Superstar*, which is all the excuse *The Sun* needs to print a picture of her proud 44-inch chest and the headline 'SUPERBUST'. Her Jesus is played by a solicitor's son from Muswell Hill called Paul Nicholas. David knows him as 'Oscar', the name he used five years ago when he made a record of one of David's early comedy songs about a prison breakout. Now he's dying on the cross to standing ovations while, streets apart, David is singing among the satellites.

Planets spin and Soho swings. Death, resurrection and *'Bong! Bong! Bong!'* Just another perfect day in August.

GEEZERS IN LIPSTICK on the Seven Sisters Road. Hard muscles in soft fabrics, smoking fags and coughing gags about looking bent and smashing faces. Hands that might have to become fists before the night is through with fingernails painted golds and blacks. Eyelids that still wink at barmaids even as they're dusted blue. Feet used to tackles in muddy boots raised on platform-heel plinths. Enough of them for a Ford assembly line, winding down the pavement outside the Rainbow Theatre, some with their birds, some without but with pupils yoyoing every sparkly bit of skirt joining the queue behind them. Just blokes who might be queer, next to dollies who don't care, next to queers who do, next to blokes who aren't, next to dollies who might be, next to queers who just look like normal blokes, next to normal blokes who just look like dollies, next to normal queers who don't even look queer, next to dollies who look like the kind of dollies blokes would try to look queer for, next to blokes who will always look more like blokes no matter how queer they dolly up.

One year ago this would have been impossible. One year ago David wasn't yet Ziggy Stardust. Now he is. Now this is what a Saturday night in London looks like.

David's face is everywhere, outside and inside, on posters, foyer hangings and souvenir programmes that come with a sheet of Ziggy cartoon skin transfers. There are transfers for 'Weird', based on Trevor, and 'Gilly', based on Woody, and 'Lady Stardust', who looks like Morticia Addams, and 'Ziggy' himself, clearly based on David. There's also a transfer for 'Starman', who looks a bit like a jelly baby with the head of Humpty Dumpty. The cartoons, drawn by David's friend George, make it very clear 'Ziggy' and 'Starman' are not the same person.

Tonight's audience of rouge-cheeked gladraggers whiffing of Us unisex deodorant and Benson & Hedges don't look much interested in skin transfers. Nor is Lou, rattling in the aisles with a triple on the rocks and a pocketful of mandies, tired bug eyes pulling focus on the flashy lapels of Elton, Rod and Jagger as they take their places as surreptitiously as their threads allow. All the stars are out, in the seats and twinkling on the painted ceiling. But all eyes, including Lou's, fix straight ahead on the stage where Roxy Music have just been and gone – not soon enough for Bryan Ferry who persevered with inflamed tonsils and a cracked tongue – and where a strange set, a bit like a building site with scaffolding planks and thin ladders, the floor covered with sawdust, awaits David's grand entrance.

It comes on the stroke of 9.30. Out of a cloud of dry ice, stepping forth in a silver paisley jumpsuit and boots to the slowly stretching piano of 'Lady Stardust'. The face of Marc suddenly appears on one of the projection screens hanging between the scaffold that boxes in the Spiders like a doll's house. As David starts to sing, bendy bodies waltz into view on the platform above, their faces hidden by masks. The face on the masks is David's. The faces beneath them belong to a dance troupe whose leader was recently described by *Time Out* magazine as *'the art of pantomime's answer to Frankie Howerd'*. The faces of the dumbstruck audience titter not.

Now David is a star he can do whatever he wants. What David now wants is the very thing that was stopping him becoming a star until he gave it up for rock'n'roll.

'Mime.'

The Lurcio in leotards is David's old 'mime' teacher, Lindsay Kemp. 'A gangbang all on his own,' as he's been known to introduce himself. In the two years since he last banged gangs with David he's been busy making films with Ken Russell, reinterpreting Jean Genet and running workshops in Covent Garden helping people to 'express emotion through gesture'. His own emotion was one of surprise when Angie contacted him out of the blue to ask if he'd collaborate on a special stage show for David's Rainbow concerts, and more surprise still when he sat down in Defries's Gunter Grove office to listen to *Ziggy Stardust* for the first time and discovered his dear old pupil with the curly hair who used to sing sweet songs about golden horses was now playing loud vulgar electric *rock* music.

David explained. He didn't expect Lindsay to be part of a *concert* but a *production*. 'The Ziggy Stardust Show' as he's always imagined it but never been able to afford until now: where rock music, pop art, fashion and 'mime' smash together as one in the greatest live spectacle ever witnessed on a modern stage. David would take care of the music and the art. Freddie would supply most of the clothes. Leaving Lindsay to choreograph the 'mime' with as many dancers as he wished. Packed houses were guaranteed along with his name on the bill and Defries's budget for all the greasepaint and jockstraps required.

Lindsay couldn't possibly refuse.

The poster lists Lindsay's company as 'The Astronettes'. On paper, it sounds suitably Ziggy. On stage, they look unsuitably *Night of the Living Dead* by Marcel Marceau. And for the next hour and a half they ruin an otherwise brilliant David Bowie gig.

As the Astronettes fandango, the background projections change: art by Warhol and Magritte, Little Richard, Marilyn Monroe, a packet of cornflakes. So does David's costume. A new one, not by Freddie but from the Fulham shop selling exclusive designs by Kansai Yamamoto: a red, one-piece, short-sleeved, legless jumpsuit decorated with woodland creatures. If nothing else, it proves he has very nice legs. He straps on an acoustic guitar and sings Jacques Brel's 'My Death' as only a man who's just been in a car crash and flown through a lightning storm can. He unstraps it for 'The Width Of A Circle', which becomes Mick's chance to shine and David's to 'mime'. If nothing else, it proves he really shouldn't. A giant glitterball is lowered for 'Starman', which briefly becomes 'Over The Rainbow' just long enough for the audience to get the punchline. Lindsay swings into view with giant wings, pretending to be stoned on an oversized joint. There are strobes, skinny figures in spiderweb leotards hanging off ladders and a noisy crescendo of 'I'm Waiting For The Man'. The stage plunges into darkness. The hesitant crowd clap for an encore. In return all they get is a curtain call so David can be presented with a giant bouquet before taking a formal bow with the rest of the ensemble.

'I thank you all very much indeed.'

And off they skip.

The house lights rise. The crowd doesn't budge. The clapping resumes. A fan clambers onto the stage, punching the air, conducting a chorus of 'WE WANT MORE!' He is swiftly bulldozed out of sight by Stuey.

The stamping and screaming continue until a loud tannoy voice, severe as the *Nine O' Clock News*, drops the bombshell.

 'David Bowie has already left the theatre!'

ROCK'N'ROLL GOES BACK TO WORK ON MONDAY. Clocking in with the *Daily Express* where Jean Rook turns on Tupperware England to lurex drainpipes and blue suede creepers from Malcolm McLaren's Let It Rock boutique. By Christmas even Cilla Black will be wearing a 'Wild Thing' T-shirt with the same leopard head as Iggy's jacket, made by the same designers, John Dove and Molly White. Style ceases to be sacred, but sex and subversion aren't so easily pulled off the peg. That's why Cilla is Cilla and Lou is Lou.

In a basement in Soho, three turns of a street corner from the theatre where Cilla last starred in panto with Basil Brush, Lou sings about a transsexual named Candy giving blow jobs. He sings it just a breath stronger than a whisper, in a warm toffee-brown lullaby voice thick with romance. Soft brushes tickle drumskin and a sleepy bass gulps up and down. The bass is really two basses playing tag, both overdubbed by David's old friend Herbie. A jazz saxophone toots, tooted by David's old saxophone teacher, Ronnie. Mick adds an Empire State sunset of sweet violins, and three Jewish backing singers nicknamed the Thunder Thighs *'doo-doo-doo'* like Times Square traffic.

'Walk On The Wild Side' might be the most New York record ever made but it is made in London, between Wardour and Dean Streets, penny arcades and peep shows, over 3,000 miles from Max's Kansas City but less than one from the nearest Angus Steak House. Lou's homesick love song to the beautiful he/she creatures of the city of night, the Hollys, Jackies, Candys and Joes, is made in the city of dilly boys, the Sombrero and a dead prostitute nicknamed 'Handbag'. Made immortal by a bisexual Brixton boy and a straight East Yorkshireman, in the perfectly gay days of August.

The television says so. 'What a gay day!' There's Larry Grayson, fresh to Friday nights on ITV dishing the dirt on Slack Alice on *Shut That Door!* And the new 'National Newspaper for Homosexuals', *Gay News*, which hopes to unify the squabbling factions of the Gay Liberation Front and the

Campaign for Homosexual Equality: one currently has a newsletter called *Come Together*, the other *Lunch*, the pity being they can't just both come together and have lunch. Beneath the streets of Soho Lou's girls *'doo-doo-doo'* as above ground the closet hinges creak. Some soft as laughter. Others loud as gunfire.

'FREEZE! THIS IS A HOLD-UP!'

Three thousand miles from Trident Studios, in the city of Holly, Jackie, Candy and Joe, in the south side of Brooklyn where a branch of the Chase Manhattan Bank sits on the corner where East Third meets with Avenue P, a man named John Wojtowicz empties around $200,000 of cash and travellers' cheques into a briefcase. It's not his money, but he desperately needs it to help his second wife. His first was a woman called Carmen. They had two kids before they separated. His second is a man called Ernie. John, in military uniform, married Ernie, in a wedding dress, in a public gay ceremony last year. Only now Ernie is in a mental hospital after trying to kill himself: he just can't stand living as a man any longer.

The money John's stuffing into his briefcase is so he can pay for Ernie's sex-change surgery. The reason the bank tellers are letting him take it is because of John's friend, Sal, who is pointing a machine gun at their chests.

The cops show up before they're out of the building. The simple robbery becomes a complicated hostage situation. The Feds roll in and by sundown John and Sal are outnumbered a hundred to one.

John demands to see Ernie. The cops bring him straight from hospital in his dressing gown. Ernie flatly refuses to see John, claiming 'he doesn't love me anymore'. Another gay friend is allowed to visit in Ernie's place. John greets him at the bank door with a kiss in full view of watching news crews and a mob of onlookers. Some cheer. Some boo.

By 3 a.m. a deal is arranged. John, Sal, the briefcase of money and two hostages are driven by limousine to Kennedy Airport where a getaway plane waits on the tarmac. The chauffeur is an FBI agent. Sal doesn't make it out of the car alive. John surrenders before they shoot him too.

Bloody news travels fast. Overnight London presses roll with front-page stories of how the crowd outside the bank had stood chanting 'Come out! Come out!' And now they have.

'GAY GUNMAN DRAMA'

'THE GAY RAID'
'GAY GANGSTERS CRAZY HOLD-UP'
Out of the closets, into the streets. The words on the newsstands in the perfect days of August when Lou takes David on his walk on the wild side.

THE OTHER DINERS try not to stare but Angie doesn't make it easy. Her short peroxide blonde hair is streaked green with vegetable dye and her voice bounces off the Grange's dark oriental furnishings like a cry for help from the bottom of a well. None of them know who she is, but a few – those in Covent Garden for *Godspell* at the Wyndham rather than *Orpheus* at the Coliseum – cast lingering glances at her dining companions.

That man there with the dyed red hair and the other one wearing glasses, the ones with that woman talking much too loudly over the scrape of silver cutlery through beef bourguignon. Is it? Yes. That's almost certainly David Bowie and Elton John – the 'Starman' man and the 'Rocket Man' man. What was that?

'JUST LIKE MARC!'

Marc Bolan, is it? What's that Bowie saying? 'Fey and prissy', was it? Whatever it was Elton doesn't look very happy, does he? Now that parrot-haired American woman's squawking, pouring more wine. Did Elton just speak? Something about best friends? Sounded like he was sticking up for Bolan. Must have been. Now Bowie doesn't look so pleased.

'OH, AND MICK TOO!'

God, that bloody woman's off again. Is that Jagger they're talking about now? 'He's my complete idol,' did Elton just say? 'If I ever met him, I'd fall in a heap and die.' Think that was it. But did Bowie laugh just then? Elton's face! Good heavens! Doesn't look like they're having that nice an evening, does it?

Oh well. Never mind them. Let's try and catch the waiter and ask for the dessert menu, shall we? I think there might just be time before curtain-up for a quick crème brûlée . . .

NOT FAR ACROSS TOWN, in an apartment block near Marble Arch with a 24-hour concierge, the sort where foreign diplomats sneak call girls in the tradesmen's entrance, Marc sits in the new flat June found them, high enough and secure enough to keep any fans at a safe distance. He is drinking champagne: the champagne from the crate Elton brought over as a gift the other night. He is listening to music: the music Jagger turned him on to a few months ago, now his favourite record, 'Clean Up Woman' by Betty Wright. The Grange restaurant is a good mile and a half away.

All of a sudden, Marc's ears start to burn.

AUGUST IS ALMOST OVER. School is still out, and so are Sandie Shaw's nipples, poking through a crocheted top on the cover of *TV Times*. Only so many perfect days left.

In Whitehall, market porters chanting 'TWO! FOUR! SIX! EIGHT! WE DON'T WANT TO INTEGRATE!' carry 'BRITAIN FOR THE BRITISH' banners to protest against the government's intake of thousands of Asians from East Africa.

In Piccadilly, Ringo takes a break from editing his film with Marc to attend the UK charity premiere of *The Godfather* while fashion pages go gangster gaga for women in pinstripe suits.

In Soho, Lou sings of sangria, parks and movies too while Mick makes piano keys sob like Chopin. In the control room, David's work is nearly done. In the studio, so is Lou's. When it is, he'll call the finished album *Transformer*.

Not perfect, but still the best anyone makes in 1972.

FIFTEEN

THE NEON SIGN is the Statue of Liberty but this is not America. This is an old bowling alley in the black-eyed suburbs of south Manchester, now a concert venue: the Hardrock. The owners spent a quarter of a million quid on turning it into 'the most modern rock complex to date'. Quadrophonic sound, coloured light shows and seats for 3,000 fans, a flick of a switch and the stage vanishes and it becomes a disco, capacity 1,500. In a city where hundreds still have to piss outside their semi-derelict cold-water slums, the Hardrock is concrete science fiction. Its promoters call themselves the Space agency. The first act to play there is David Bowie and The Spiders From Mars.

Trouble is, they're not so big on aliens round these parts. It's cos of all these 'bloody Pakis' coming in from Uganda, the ones being ejected by that 'Black Hitler' Idi Amin. The same ones those porters in London were marching about. There've been letters sent out telling folk if they've got a spare bedroom in the house then by law they're going to have to take in 'a whole family of Pakis'. The letters say they're from the council. They're not. It's a shit-stirring hoax on behalf of anti-immigration groups. The anonymous jackbooters responsible swear they're 'not racialist'. They just think this government 'is too soft'. So does the front page of the *Daily Express*.

'NO NEED TO LET THEM IN'

So do the readers of the *Manchester Evening News*.

'*It is about time that this government put a stop to the many thousands of immigrants coming to stay in this country. We are just a dumping ground for the whole world.*'

Manchester isn't alone. They're just as petrified in London, Birmingham, Sheffield and every other city in England being told the Patels, Choudhurys and Chatterjees are coming for your house, your job, your wife, your kids and your cat and dog for their stinking curry. But at least Manchester has solved the problem of racial tensions.

'Laughter,' local funnyman Bernard Manning tells *The Sun*. 'Pakis love to laugh at coloured jokes.'

Go on?

'Hear about the Yorkshireman who wanted to convert this Paki? He kicked him over the bar and converted him for Leeds.'

And they laughed all the way back to Africa.

On stage at the Hardrock, David sparkles in the spotlight clothed in exotic fabrics chosen by Freddie and Daniella from Bangladeshi markets in London's East End. There is a silver bangle on his wrist and daubs of colour on his face. He's as queer-looking a foreign bugger as ever dared to show his face in Stretford on match day. The alien's alien. His two nights here are a complete sell-out with hundreds more kids turned away at the door.

For Manchester, for England, for the planeloads of Ugandan Asians flying in with their passports ripped, possessions stolen, some with faces scarred from being 'shaved' with broken beer bottles by Amin's goon squads – just maybe, there is hope.

SEVEN YEARS AGO, Pete Townshend didn't mind other guys dancing with his girl down the Goldhawk Club in Shepherd's Bush. Seven years on, David kicks 'The Kids Are Alright' up a postcode to Kensington and down the stairs of the Sombrero. The Queers are Alright, but David's boy isn't.

'*Oh, lordy!*'

It's his new single, 'John, I'm Only Dancing', a bisexual disco drama buzzing from the King's Road jukebox of Let It Rock, like the sound of a homi-polone catfight in lurex drainpipes. You don't have to be gay to love it, but it helps. This explains why none of his usual friendly press critics do. Luckily, Alan Freeman does. 'You Don't Mess Around With Jim', 'Suzanne, Beware Of The Devil', 'John, I'm Only Dancing'. It's all the same after-school pick of the pops to Fluff, who's been playing it every afternoon on Radio 1 as his Record of the Week.

'Not 'arf!'

Beneath the neon, down the stairs, the Sombrero doesn't change. It just becomes more so. The lips more glossy, the eyes more glassy, the queens more draggy, the mandies more druggy, the decadence more divine. So long as angry boots keep marching through London streets with banners for Enoch, the Sombrero will always be its Kit Kat Klub.

'*Willkommen! Bienvenue! Welcome!*'

Still Amadeo on the door, still Antonello on the decks, still limp salads in every booth and stiff glances from slinky waiters, still pursed lips and champagne teeth, still boyish hips grinding on the illuminated dartboard-like dancefloor, still Aretha's 'Spanish Harlem' and Melanie's 'Lay Down', still Freddie looking fabulous, still Daniella dazzling, still Angie outraging, still glitter bitch eyes pretending not to care how famous David has become.

Still Wendy swishing into David's booth in something crepe by Ossie Clark. He leans over and coyly grabs his chance to ask what she thinks of Mott's 'All The Young Dudes'; he'd mentioned her and Freddie by name, joking how she steals her clothes from Marks & Spencer. Wendy wants to say she loves it. She wants to say she loves *him*. But the Sombrero house rules of the piss-elegant game forbid sincerity. She sets her face to glacial blasé.

'Oh, that? You could at least have made it Harrods.'

And swishes away before her mask cracks with regret.

David, silent, expressionless, leans back against red velvet. All around him, the old-time ambassadors of 'Queen Bitch', the funky little boat races of 'All The Young Dudes', the pretty Annies and Joes of 'John, I'm Only Dancing'. He empties his glass and lights a cigarette. The gay bright young things dance on, David watching them through the gauze of his smoke like tropical fish through dirty glass. With no idea for certain when he'll be seeing them again.

★

THERE ARE AS MANY KIDS on the roof of Heathrow Airport as can fit in the Hardrock. Three thousand of them, all here to wave him off to America, every one screaming his name.

'DAAAAAVID!'

From the observation balconies, he is just a tiny dot on the tarmac surrounded by other tiny dots of policemen and bodyguards. He tries to talk to them on a megaphone. They can't hear him over their own screams. He gives up, waves one last time, then scarpers up the steps to board his plane.

David Cassidy is glad to be going home.

He's spent the last five days living on a yacht moored in the Thames, here on a press trip to promote his new single 'How Can I Be Sure' and set up a tour for next year. The yacht, the 120-foot *Ocean Sabre*, was a £2,000 security measure to keep fans away. It didn't stop two of them jumping off Tower Pier to try to swim to him before the River Police fished them out. The ones who didn't risk drowning still stayed there all night, every night, chanting his name. On board, Cassidy could hear them in his cabin, keeping him awake. Just as he can still hear them now at 40,000 feet on a Boeing 747, in his skull, vibrating the echo chamber between his eyeballs loud and shrill as a circular saw.

'DAAAAAVID!'

There are many hours left before Los Angeles. There will be twice as many drinks.

As Cassidy hurtles through the troposphere, somewhere far below, visible from his plane window as no more than a faint white speck in the vast Atlantic ocean, the world's largest ship in terms of gross tonnage, the luxury liner *Queen Elizabeth 2*, is on the second day of its voyage to New York. In one of its most expensive cabin suites, with walls of Thai cotton, beige carpets, caramel curtains, oak veneer furniture and check upholstery in mauve and aquamarine, another pop singer named David dresses for dinner.

He and Angie have several restaurants to choose from. Lamb cutlets in the blue tweed banquettes of the Britannia. Filet Mignon Béarnaise behind the bronze-tinted glass of the Columbia. Supreme of Turbot Chablis on the Bordeaux red leather of the Grill Room. Whichever they choose, heads will twirl and ogle mid-forkful of Broccoli Polonaise. David's hair will clash with the trellised ceiling, his clothes with the mother of pearl statuettes, his shoes with the olive-green carpet. But seven days of funny looks, seasickness and no newspaper to read other than the *Daily Telegraph* is better than seven hours on a plane spending every second convinced that in the next you are definitely going to die.

Behind him, already hundreds of nautical miles out of sight, is an island nation adjusting its back-to-school ears to Marc's new single, 'Children Of The Revolution', and its work-weary eyes to the new series of *Love Thy Neighbour*. The titles roll on Monday night at 8.30 p.m. The first 'sambo' pings out of Eddie Booth's gob at 8.32. The first 'nig-nog' at 8.33. History will not favour *Love Thy Neighbour*, but a *TV Times* audience survey does; in 1972 it ranks the second most popular programme in a poll of black households. 'This show is about integration,' argues its producer-director Stuart Allen. 'We want to cool things and we think we're going to succeed.' Success being a piss-poor copy of the BBC's *Till Death Us Do Part* for those intellectually stretched by the original. Those who aren't will be glad to see Alf Garnett also back on the box this week. 'No writer can change the world,' says Alf's creator, Johnny Speight. 'The only thing he can do is to bring things to light. People used to say that Britain didn't have a colour bar. But there it's been, lying dormant all the time.' For Speight, Alf is a grotesque bigoted buffoon to be laughed at, not with. 'I feel sorry for him. I mean, a working-class man who votes Tory?' But three days after Alf returns to TV screens the Tory Monday Club stage a 'Halt Immigration Now' rally in Westminster Central Hall. Over 2,000 real-life Booths and Garnetts attend. By the end of September, *Till Death Us Do Part* will be the number 1 programme in the national ratings. Number 2, of course, is *Love Thy Neighbour*.

Sail on, David. Sail as far away from this septic isle as you possibly can.

SIXTEEN

THE STATUE IS THE STATUE OF LIBERTY.

This is America. And this, David, is the Hudson River, and that is Pier 94. This is your reception committee. These are your old friends from *Pork*, capable Zee, lovable Leee and vivacious Cherry Vanilla. That's Barbara, the secretary of your label boss Dennis at RCA, and this funny old chap is called Gustl Breuer, their 57-year-old Austrian promotions man who'll be chaperoning you throughout your stay. This is the limousine waiting to chauffeur you the short distance to the Plaza Hotel. These are the Bavarian frescoes and chandeliers of the Oak Room. Those are welcoming flutes of champagne. That is your manager Tony Defries, who you'd recognise even without a Cuban cigar screwed in his face. This is a bellhop, that is an elevator to the eighth floor and this is your suite looking north over Central Park. That is the king-size bed, should you want to roll around its sheets with your wife, or anyone else. That is the telephone should you need more Moët from room service. This is the television should you choose to watch tonight's *Columbo* with guest murderer John Cassavetes. That is the front page of today's *New York Times* with Democrat nominee George McGovern accusing President Nixon of a 'whitewash' in his investigation of the Watergate break-in. No two ways about it, David. *This* is America.

'*David Bowie, unofficial leader of the rock and rouge movement, arrived in New York for his first public appearance on these shores . . . by ship. He is afraid of flying, but not of cruising.*'

And this is the hype in *Andy Warhol's Interview* magazine that spread from a duplex on East 58th Street – a horn's beep from the exit of the Queensboro Bridge, just a few blocks north of Garbo – where Defries has set up Mainman, New York. Much like Gunter Grove, but topsy-turvy so upstairs is the office, downstairs his and Melanie's apartment. Zee found the place, furnished the place and staffed the place with his friends including Cherry and Leee. In return for $100 a week, free limousines and a charge account for all their meals and drinks at Max's Kansas City, Defries expects every one of them to dedicate every second of their lives fanatically convincing the rest of America that David is already a Stateside superstar. A job made difficult only by the fact he isn't.

The week he arrives, David is less popular in America than Gary Glitter, who has a Top 10 hit with 'Rock And Roll Part 2'. David has none. In the album chart, Rod, Elton and even Gilbert O'Sullivan are all in the Top 10. *Ziggy* is way down at number 121. He's had the local *Sunday News* call him *'The Elvis of the Seventies'* and this week's ads in *The Village Voice* announcing him as *'The Incredible David Bowie'*, but you'd be chucking an awful lot of darts before you hit anyone on the streets of New York City in September 1972 who knew who the fuck David Bowie was.

'David who?'

Mike Garson doesn't.

'David Bowie,' says the smooth voice on the other end of the line. 'He's a big rock star from England.'

Big? Garson likes the sound of big. Big means money. More money than the $5 he earned last night playing jazz piano on the Upper West Side to a full house of oxygen. More money than the few dollars he'll get right now trying to teach piano lessons in his small Brooklyn apartment while his laughing two-year-old daughter pinballs off his shelves of books on music and Dianetics. Garson could do with some big in his life.

'And the audition's when, you say?'

'How soon can you get to RCA on West 44th and Sixth?'

The receiver to his ear, Garson's eyes switch from his daughter to his patient pupil and back again. Daughter, pupil. Daughter, pupil. Daughter, babysitter. Surely they wouldn't mind?

'Gimme a half-hour.'

Garson arrives at the studio in the same dungarees and check shirt he was wearing when he picked up the phone. He is met by a handsome blond man in shiny trousers with a soft face and a funny accent he struggles to understand who ushers him to a waiting piano. Through the glass in the control booth he sees who he assumes to be the big rock star from England he's never heard of. At least he dresses like a big rock star. Freaky hair, loud clothes, altogether pretty kooky, but then he'd have to be to call on Garson. The man on the phone, his manager Tony somebody or other, said something about Annette Peacock. Garson played piano on a couple of tracks on her latest RCA album, *I'm The One*. It's a deranged album by a deranged singer which only seriously deranged people would enjoy. The man on the phone said the big rock star from England enjoyed it, which is why Garson's here. Peacock recommended him. None of which really adds up. The deranged avant-garde wailings of Annette Peacock and big English rock stars? Maybe this is all some dreadful mix-up.

Garson sits down at the keys. The blond man hands him sheet music of a song he's never heard called 'Changes'. He places it on the stand in front of him. He reads the music in his head, as it is, lines and dots in black and white. Then his fingers play it in colour. Playing it like Pollock paints it, splattering chords against the keys so they drip onto the floor, making the music streak in silvers over action sloshes of blacks, whites, yellows and reds, but never losing focus on the tune.

'OK, OK!'

The blond man stops him.

Garson's been playing for all of eight seconds. By the tenth he's thinking how bad he must be to have blown an audition so quickly.

The blond man speaks again. 'You've gorrit.'

'Pardon?'

'You've got it,' smiles Mick. 'The gig's yours!'

In Brooklyn, Sue Garson arrives home a little shocked to find her daughter Jennifer being looked after by a total stranger. She prepares dinner rehearsing all the angry reprimands she'll have for her husband when he walks back through the door. They remain unsaid. Instead, he'll burst in with a hug and a kiss and tell her he's now on $800 a week playing piano for the big English rock star David Bowie. And Sue will

111

light up, and hug and kiss him back, even as her smile fractures with the tiniest of frowns.

'David who?'

DAVID JOHANSEN. He's the one who looks like Jagger wearing drag, only better-looking than when the real Jagger wears drag. The one with legs like bobby pins and more hair than the three Ronettes put together calls himself Johnny Thunders. The small tarted-up Marc lookalike is Sylvain Sylvain. The not-quite-so-tarted-up Marc lookalike is Billy Murcia. The tall deadpan one who looks like a transvestite axe murderer is, appropriately enough, Arthur 'Killer' Kane. Five kids from the five boroughs with enough attitude to sink Rikers Island, each exercising their divine birthright to stand on stage and take whatever blows fate throws at them for daring to be the New York Dolls.

They've been together less than a year, long enough for *Andy Warhol's Interview* to call them *'subterranean flash sleazoid rock'*. It's the second best thing anyone's ever said about them. The best was eight weeks ago when they were given a whole page in *Melody Maker* thanks to the gobsmacked fervour of its New York correspondent, Roy Hollingworth, a bright and beaky bon vivant who until being sent to America lived with Barrie and his stickered doctor's bag above Pizza Express in Dean Street. Roy's article began, *'They might just be the best rock and roll band in the world,'* and ended, *'they're just the best new young band I've ever seen.'* Words to make anyone desperate to hear the New York Dolls, even if practically nobody who read it was able to since they've yet to sign a record deal. The only way to hear them is the same way Roy did. Live in the lipsticked flesh in their twice-weekly residency at a converted hotel in Greenwich Village, now the labyrinthine Mercer Arts Center where the Dolls have just outgrown its small cabaret-sized Oscar Wilde Room for the larger, tier-seated O'Casey Theater. And where, tonight, as Johansen sashays up and down rasping Bo Diddley, he gazes out across a crowd not so full that he doesn't twig the skinny dude with the red hair and paisley jumpsuit as being that David Bowie guy.

The Dolls know who David is, but then they would. Cut them and they bleed Stones, Kinks and Pretty Things. They're unapologetic

Anglosluts who always read the cool English music papers, which is why they still can't believe any cool English music paper would want to write about *them*.

It's because they did that David knows who the Dolls are too. He read Roy's *Maker* feature two months back, unaware his friend Leee, now working for Mainman, was the unnamed photographer who took the portrait that ran with it. Thanks to Leee's invitation, now they're in front of him and Angie, defying his eyes and ears to nail them down as any one thing or the other. The style is a bit Iggy, a bit Alice, but then again really nothing like either. The sound is a bit early Stones, a bit T. Rex, but then again maybe something else. They wear vampy make-up, blouses and heels, and their songs could almost be girl group songs, if girl groups sang about Vietnam, drugs and fucking Frankenstein's monster. David can't decide. All he knows is they're as New York as a steaming manhole cover and as rock'n'roll as Little Richard's pancake.

So are their audience. The same beautiful heads rattling with fucked-up minds you'll see down Max's Kansas City hanging out with Lou's muses.

Angie knows David's eyes well enough to spot her two blinks before he does. Through no fault of her own she was born Kathleen Hetzekian. Now she calls herself Cyrinda Foxe, and she chose well. Cyrinda – which even Mary Whitehouse couldn't say without making it sound sexy – and Foxe as in *foxxxy laydeh*. Cyrinda Foxe is as sexily Cyrinda and foxily Foxe as it's possible for a woman to be. People tell her she looks like Marilyn, which she does: a subterranean sleazoid flash Marilyn. That's why she's here at the Mercer dancing to the Dolls. That's why she goes out with their singer.

Much as David is their honoured guest, when he meets them after the show it is to their world he must descend. Traffic doesn't flow up the other way. The more they talk, the more the manhole cover steams. David's senses tingle just as they did when he first met Lou and Iggy. Seductive danger. Or in Cyrinda's case, seductive seduction. When David says 'hello' the sexual tension is immediate. Any thicker and you could scoop it up in a cocktail glass and stick an olive on top. Angie can taste it, so can Johansen, but this is deep downtown New York, baby, and anything goes.

'HEY! I WANNA EAT YOUR CUNT!'

The yell of a passing trucker welcomes David to the Bowery. Of all the gin joints in all the world, the Dolls would have to take him for an aftershow drink at the Canal Street Center Rest. There are dive bars and dive bars but this dives so low it's smacked its head unconscious on the bottom. The booze is so cheap you'd be as well to wash in it. The regulars look as if they do: once a year. This is the face, more scars than teeth, of the real New York, a whole different planet from the Rockefeller playpark of gold taps and red carpets uptown at the Plaza, where a dead body in an alleyway is just another lucky bum's chance to steal some shoes.

David numbs his fears with a double shot of sleaze. When the limo finally takes him back to the hotel he'll be splayed in the backseat snuggled next to Cyrinda. So will Angie, clutching hands with sleepy Billy Doll. Together, they'll get out and clamber up the Plaza's carpeted steps, into the elevator and then the different rooms of their suite where what will happen will happen. And in the morning Angie will say what a 'FABULOUS' time they all had. And isn't Cyrinda her new 'SWEETIE'. And isn't David still her 'DARLING'. And isn't Angie trying to keep a smile on her face just a little too hard?

THE GREYHOUND BUS ROLLS WEST out of New York City. Sal Paradise o'clock. David is *On the Road*. So is Angie, though they don't sit together, and David's friend George and his wife Birgit, here purely for company. There is Defries and his girlfriend Melanie, and Zee, who without volunteering has been appointed tour manager, and Mainman's official photographer Mr Rock and his wife Sheila. There is the band, Mick, Trevor and Woody, and their new pianist, Garson. There is Suzy, in charge of hair and wardrobe, and Robin the sound man, and Pete the stage manager and his assistant Willie, and the lighting crew of Bob, Jim and Steve. There is the new three-man security detail of tasty Tony, David's wheeler-dealer downstairs neighbour whose wife Sue is looking after Zowie back in Beckenham, and Stuey, and another tall ebony afroed Adonis named Anton. There are long hours of numbing flat scenery, infinite highways, service stations and stiff sleep. There is singing and strumming, blue jokes and cigarettes, cans of beer and bottles of Scotch, the grinding of marijuana and the silent popping of Quaaludes to the back of the throat. There are windows like postcards of blue skies, that become cinema screens of sunsets, that become mirrors of night. There is the inescapable contagion of diesel madness that spares no one.

David's first concert on American soil is in Cleveland, Ohio, the city that thinks it's the birthplace of rock'n'roll: where one local paper welcomes him with the headline *'New rock singer: Bowie or girl?'*, and where thanks to months of support from local radio station WMMS he manages to fill and thrill all 3,000 seats of the smaller of its two Music Halls.

His second is in Memphis, Tennessee, the city that knows it's the birthplace of rock'n'roll: where Elvis isn't home the night David's red boots tread the same boards his white bucks once scuffed in Ellis Auditorium and where, as in Cleveland, the manic crowd fool him into believing conquering America will be a cinch.

His third is back in New York, New York, the city that might as well be the birthplace of rock'n'roll: where a single klieg light brushes the stars above West 57th Street next to the words 'FALL IN LOVE WITH DAVID BOWIE' hanging above Carnegie Hall. You play here and you chisel yourself into history next to the names of Benny Goodman, Frank Sinatra and Judy Garland, or so they say. Things didn't quite work out that way for Marc when T. Rex played here seven months ago. Marc had klieg lights too, and just as much press hype as RCA have been puffing ahead of David's performance. All it got him was a headline in the following day's *New York Times* which read 'NO. 1 BRITISH ROCK GROUP FAILS TO LIVE UP TO ITS PUBLICITY'. Carnegie Hall is where legends are either made or destroyed, and it spat Marc back on the sidewalk quicker than a wise guy's spent toothpick.

The capacity of its main auditorium is less than the Manchester Hardrock. The day of David's concert the New York papers still carry 'A Few Seats Remaining' ads. Defries and RCA are adamant there won't be an empty one in the house, even if they have to give tickets away. Which they do.

The firing squad of American critics are all here, muskets raised, and so are the British. Jackie O's sister Lee Radziwill is here, and *Psycho's* Anthony Perkins, and *Women in Love's* Alan Bates, and Andy Warhol, missing Lou who would be here too if he wasn't gigging in England, and

David's new friends the Dolls and Cyrinda. And every other painted-faced, blue-haired, see-thru-bloused, glittery-nailed, pasted-feathered, wild-wigged, snakeskin-heeled and golden-sequined creature of the New York night expecting to see England's answer to Alice Cooper, the transvestite Elvis, the crown prince of fag rock or whoever else those who actually paid for a ticket believe they're getting for their $6.50.

What they get is the carefully coordinated theatricality the Perelman Stage expects. Strobes, Beethoven and clang went the trolley. Red boots, silver suits and ding goes the bell. Guitar blowjobs, blown kisses and zing go the heart strings. From the moment it sees David, Carnegie falls.

His voice is hampered by a head cold incubated during too many days boxed in on a Greyhound bus, but not so noticeable that anyone can tell. The same *Times* critic who called Marc *'an illusion of style with an almost total lack of substance'* will conclude *'as a performer, Bowie delivered'*. The reporters for the five British pop weeklies, including Roy from the *Maker*, agree. David takes Manhattan as Marc never could.

There's a lot of it to take. At the after-party in the Plaza, sex comes to David as easy as inhaling a cigarette, and what he can't inhale others will. Girls of indeterminate youth who might be just out of college or just out of braces linger, waiting to be hoovered up by men old enough to spot the difference and lusty enough not to ask. Almost everyone fucks almost anyone. Because this is what some people call rock'n'roll.

Because it sounds better than calling it what it actually is.

SEVENTEEN

BA-DA-DA BOMP BOMP BOMP!

It starts as a tour bus singalong based on the holy sound of Bo Diddley, based on the old testament of Muddy Waters, based on the hoodoo moans of the sons and grandsons of men and women with scarred fingers and broken backs and vengeful faith. Like they can hear it, echoing in the blood-soaked soil beneath the green plains of Tennessee and Kentucky as their Greyhound rolls by, loud enough that they start humming with the throaty rhythm of black ghosts. But being white boys raised on the wails of Wardour Street, they speed it up, just like the Yardbirds did, from a deep grind to a quick jerk. *Ba-da-da bomp bomp bomp. Ba-da-da bomp bomp bomp.* They know it's not their riff, nor the Yardbirds', nor Bo's, nor Muddy's, but something older than electricity.

It becomes David's.

The road writes the music and the city the words. New York blows David like a horn and out of his mouth snap phrases like bubblegum. Pure jet boy jive the colour of Cyrinda's lipstick, sticky as a Bowery john floor, cool as a skirt-raising subway breeze on Lexington and 52nd, about Iggy and nobody, Manhattan and nowhere, sheet-scratching sex and absolutely nothing. David will say it's his song but it's all Gotham's, apart from the title. A nod to his old friend Lindsay who he wanted to bring to America to tour the same theatrical show they'd performed at the Rainbow, until

117

Defries ruled it logistically impractical and financially impossible. The last he heard, Lindsay was thinking of reviving his earlier production called *Flowers*, based on the work of Jean Genet, casting himself as the main character, Divine, a homosexual drag queen. It's David's little joke. Steal the riff of 'I'm A Man' and stick it in a wig called 'The Jean Genie'.

The muse strikes him between shaking sheets on West 59th. Days later he records it between vibration eliminators on West 44th. In the smallest of RCA's main in-house studios, Studio D, its acoustics specially designed for hard rock groups, The Spiders play as hard as they ever have, as hard as they always could but were never asked. 'The Jean Genie' demands it. Urgent, simple, don't think just fuck. They make a sound like a frying rattlesnake, in short sharp spits of venom and burning fat, so hot Trevor misses his cue for the first chorus but so fierce David keeps his fumble in the mix. Any other studio in any other city it wouldn't sound the same. As it is, as it was meant to be, oh, David – you beautiful New York Doll!

SOMEWHERE MIDWEST. It could be St Louis. Maybe Kansas. It doesn't make a lot of difference because one five-star hotel room is much like another. The sealed windows with a skyline view, the thick floor-to-ceiling curtains, the large soft bed, the gentle purr of the air con, the remote-control television, the walnut writing desk, the smooth bedside lamp, the sparkling telephone.

Dai picks up the receiver and dials. He waits, listening to the American ring tone, thinking how different it is from the English ring tone. Until the leisurely voice of Defries answers with a simple 'Hello?'

Defries is still in New York. So is David and the rest of the band and crew, killing time before the next two dates in Chicago and Detroit. The tour was put together through the William Morris Agency, who initially set up just eight concerts across four weeks. Now Defries has sacked them, convinced he can do a better job of booking more dates himself. The fact he's never arranged a tour before and has only limited first-hand knowledge of America won't stop him. He has everything he thinks he needs. A telephone and a map. All that's missing is a blindfold and a pin. The method is the same. Pick a state, then a city, then a venue, then a local promoter, then send either of his two 'advance men', Dai or

Leee, ahead to double-check the auditorium and sow some much-needed publicity. As old-fashioned and straightforward as it is utterly naïve.

Somewhere Midwest, it's Dai's turn to be David's pied piper. His main task is to find the most influential DJs at the local radio station and invite them and their partners, and maybe the station boss and his wife, and maybe the chief entertainment reporter from the local paper as well, all out for a slap-up dinner, always in the restaurant attached to whichever fancy hotel Defries has asked RCA's travel department to book Dai into.

Rule number one: *never* eat anywhere else.

The deal is that the jocks and the hacks and their lady friends can scoff as many courses and guzzle all the champagne they want while Dai reiterates just how marvellous it would be if they could all get behind David ahead of his coming concert in their city with plenty of airplay on WW-Whatever-Initials FM and lots of fat column inches in whatever their *Tribune Star Post-Dispatch Sentinel Examiner* may be. Which is surely the least they can do after Dai picks up the bill.

Rule number two: *always* add the bill to the room.

Rule number three: when you check out of the hotel, sign *everything* to be paid by 'RCA Records & Tapes'.

Whether RCA Records & Tapes have actually agreed to pay for any of this is known only to Defries. Dai often wonders but knows better than to ask. Better to follow the rules and say nothing. Until you can't hold your tongue any longer.

'Tony? It's Dai. Listen, could you wire me over some cash?'

'Cash?'

'Yeah. I dunno, maybe $20 or something? See, I don't have any actual cash on me.'

'What do you need cash for?'

'Oh, you know, just so I can get some breakfast.'

'What do you mean?'

'You know, like a few dollars to get some breakfast across the street.'

'They don't do breakfast in the hotel?'

'Yes.'

'Then have breakfast there.'

'But their breakfast is ten dollars. If I go over the road, it's only two or three dollars.'

'So?'

'So I thought it'd save money.'

'That's what the room charge is for.'

'So you don't mind?'

'No. You don't need cash.'

'But it seems a waste of money.'

'It's not your money. I've already told you. Bill back everything to RCA.'

'Everything?'

'Everything. Don't worry about the cost, just stick it all on the bill like we agreed. Is that it?'

'Yes.'

'Good. Any problems with the venue, call me back.'

'OK . . .'

The line goes dead. Dai blows through his lips like a deflating balloon and scratches his forehead. His eyes take another roam around the room. The skyline view, the curtains, the bed, the air con, the television, the writing desk, the lamp, the telephone. And not two dimes in his jeans. He laughs, pushing down the hook switch then punching a button. After a few seconds a bright American voice says, 'Hello! How may I help you?'

'Room service? This is Mr Davies in 442 . . .'

WHO ARE YOU, DAVID? The microphones of America wiggle under your nose like a pack of excitable puppies. Go on, throw them some bones. Give them something that'll have them running back to their editors for a tickle on the belly. What do you say?

'I'm not what I'm supposed to be.'

Like some of that pre-tour publicity you read about yourself which made you out to be part of some new wave intelligentsia. That's not you. You're not an intellectual by any stretch of the imagination. You're not a primitive either, though. You're a tactile thinker. You pick up on things. But you don't really want your audience to *think* anything when they see you. They're probably just as confused about your writing as you are. You're the last one to understand most of the material you write. You have a strong lyrical emotional drive but you're not sure if that's really *you* who's coming through in the songs. They come out and you hear them afterwards and think, 'Well, whoever wrote that felt strongly about it.' But you yourself can't ever feel that strongly. You get numb. You think you're a pretty cold person, don't you? A *very* cold person. A bit of an iceman. Go on, tell them.

'Off stage, I'm a robot.'

That's why you adopted Ziggy on stage, isn't it? Only now you feel more and more like this monster and less like 'David Bowie', never mind David Jones. You've forgotten who that is. Because it's only on stage you achieve emotion. It's why you prefer being Ziggy to David. You play roles. Fragments of yourself. That's why you think of yourself as an actor rather than a rock artist.

'I have very rarely felt like a rock artist.'

You don't even think that's much of a vocation, being a rock'n'roller. You're not into *being*, you're into *performing*. The way you see it, very few countries need rock'n'roll. Very few. Only really America and England, and maybe Germany. Rock'n'roll provides a family life that is missing there. A sense of community, which is what it gave you. That's why when you were a boy you were always fascinated with America. You read Jack Kerouac's *On the Road* and it was the most important thing that ever happened to you. And now you're on that same road, your name in their newspapers, your face in their magazines, your songs on their radio.

'But now that I'm here I've forgotten why I wanted to come.'

So why did you? Is it for the fame? The money? The sex? Is this really what it all boils down to? Applause, dollars and pussy? Is that what all this is about? Or is it all just part of the act?

And if it is, then what *is* the act? Are you starring in the tragedy of the boy born David Jones or the comedy of the man who would be Ziggy Stardust? And do you even know yourself?

'There's a lot of confusions in my general make-up . . . I feel as though I'm on a tightrope more and more . . . a kind of precipice.'

Seriously. *Who* are you, David?

ANGIE COULD TELL HIM. She knows David better than himself. Where he hurts and how to kiss it better. How to put a smile on his face easy as running his bath and pouring his orange juice. What he needs and who to terrorise to get it. What he dreams and how to make them come true. That's why he always needed her.

Needed.

And now, thanks to her, the dreams have come true. They were his dreams, but still *their* dreams, because they made them happen, together. That was their pact, deeper than love.

And now?

And now an open marriage blows the doors off its hinges, much wider for some than for others. And now Cyrinda. And now the jailbait brides of Dracula. And now the sleazy aftershow cliché. And now Mister Bisexual Enigma of the 'gay rock revolution' becomes just another estuary rock star humping his way through starfuckme teenage America.

And now past the point of humiliation. And now enough. And now the goose throws a knockout punch back in the gander's face.

It happens down south. In the public swimming pool of a stopover motel, late at night but illuminated by the poolside lights so anyone watching can plainly see Angie's head dipping up and down above the waterline. Riding Anton the big Jamaican bodyguard.

David is mortified. The tour crew are embarrassed. The hotel staff are appalled.

Defries is secretly delighted. Such amazing disgrace. It's the chance he's been waiting for to send Angie's interfering windpipe packing back home to England, out of his way, exactly where he wants her. David doesn't try to stop him. Or her. She leaves the next day.

Whereas Anton stays with the tour. But that's just how it goes in rock'n'roll. Whatever happens on the road, guys gotta stick together.

EIGHTEEN

AS YOU ROLL SLOWLY UP THE CURVED DRIVE, past palm trees fat as pineapples and tall as tower cranes, it looks like a gay millionaire's wedding cake. A giant H-shaped slab smothered in pink icing. A thick slice would be so sweet it'd probably make you sick. If you could afford it. For those who can, the Beverly Hills Hotel is Heaven on Earth. For those who can't just sign it all off to 'RCA Records & Tapes'.

The scent of tropical plants, cologne, sun oil and cigars that cost more to import than their Cuban rollers' salary. The sound of lazy splashing, tinkling ice and groggy loungers being paged by the pool where a waiter will bring a telephone to your green-clothed table on an extension lead long as the Mississippi. The surrounding peach-pink stucco makes the blue sky seem bluer, the yellow roses yellower, the red azaleas redder, the orange bird of paradise flowers more orangey and reality a fast-fading memory.

The perfect place to be when reality is a tour that went bankrupt last week.

The combined loose change of the whole crew can barely scrape to one daiquiri in the Polo Lounge where the whole crew can barely move for bellies full of steak and lobster. They're here because David's playing two sold-out nights at the 3,000-capacity Santa Monica Civic Auditorium. The box office won't cover their bar tab. If they really need money to spend elsewhere, they can always beg Zee for a per diem, or pick up tourists who'll gladly pay them dollars to eat hotel meals the crew can stick on their room. Cash or credit, either way everything's free.

Behind the main building, David has his own exclusive bungalow, Elizabeth Taylor's favourite, number 5, with its own private pool. He doesn't dip a toe.

Elton is also here, staying in the bungalow next door: with two sell-out nights at the 18,000-capacity LA Forum and an album in the US Top 10, he can afford Beverly Hills. David is currently number 144.

You wouldn't know it to walk into the new club opposite the Chateau Marmont where skinny Lolitas shake tie-front blouses to 'Suffragette City' thinking they're the cat's meow. So does the gonky little man like a squashed Rod Stewart spinning the discs. The E Club is where the Sunset Strip gets to dream it's the King's Road between the hours of 6 p.m. and 2 a.m. and none dream wetter than David's old friend Rodney, playing the tunes to pull the chicks to pull the bands who play the tunes to pull the chicks. To David's crew he's the candyman, dishing out sweets to order like a courtesan pick'n'mix. This, too, is what some people call rock'n'roll. Like screwing a groupie at one end of a restaurant table while the people sat at the other are enjoying their drinks. These things happen because when nothing costs, nothing has value, nothing is real.

All is pornography.

A LEOPARD'S HEAD hangs over the back of a chair in Western Recorders. The music buzzing the speakers sounds just like it. White-fanged, bloody-mouthed and psycho-eyed. Wild animal music always stalking for the next kill. Primal rhythms, flesh-stripping guitars and hot snarls about sick boys, savage girls, napalm and penetration. The kind of words a leopard would sing. Or a *'streetwalkin' cheetah'* if you want it to scan better.

David pushes a fader. A guitar gargles and a human screams.

'Is that OK, Jim?'

Iggy nods. David pushes another.

There are just the two of them, Ziggy and Iggy, David and Jim, sat in front of an old mixing board in a small room in a big flat concrete building far along Sunset Boulevard. The music is the album Iggy's just finished recording in London before flying out to join David. It's not quite as rough as the first demos he made earlier in the summer, but not so smooth to change Defries's opinion that the new Stooges aren't fit for public consumption. David has been asked to play with the master tapes to try to tweak a better mix than the one Iggy's presented. Iggy doesn't object and couldn't even if he wanted to. Either David mends it or Defries bins it.

There's not a lot to play with. The band can't be separated as they're all on the one track. James's lead guitar is on another, Iggy's vocals on a third. The best David can do is add a little echo here, isolate the odd lick and compress the rest into as hard a box around the ears as its vicious energy demands. The truth is he can't fix what isn't broken, just as he can't make clean what's meant to sound as filthy as four bobcats fucking in a junkyard. This is a brave new rock'n'roll, even braver than the Dolls, who love it too much to undo it the way Iggy does, disconnecting its past, attacking its present, challenging its future.

Outside on the Strip it's still only October '72. There's a giant billboard for the debut album by the Eagles, who last month told a New York crowd in the wake of David's recent visit that they weren't one of 'those sissy groups'.

Inside with *Raw Power*, it's already '77.

DAVID IS SOMEWHERE BETWEEN. His music just in today, his clothes far ahead in tomorrow. Since he's been touring the States he's adopted a new style to match the street tough vibrations of the Dolls and Iggy that won't leave his head: tight jeans with half-mast turn-ups, studded leather belts and a short fur-collared metallic-blue bomber jacket, always worn bare-chested. With a choker chain around his neck it makes him look what any trigger-happy LAPD cop would call a real punk.

He's become a whole new Ziggy, harder and scarier, not the light dreamy Ziggy of 'Starman' but the dirty sex Ziggy of 'The Jean Genie' and the other songs he's been writing on the road about jerks, dealers, guns, hookers and the American darkness always to be found before dawn's early light. Five weeks in, with each day that passes he becomes more infected by the country's secret chaos, its absurd enormity, its blindness to its own unbearable loneliness. The Greyhound since ditched, while the rest of the crew fly from state to state, David's been travelling by train, spending hours in the observation car hypnotised by deserts, mountain ridges, reservoirs, empty drive-ins and lifeless farms, pick-up trucks with 'NIXON NOW' stickers, billboards for Schlitz and mile after mile of telegraph poles, each stark as a crucifix ready for Roman justice. And at the end of each track, another fast mad city completely at odds with the slow sad land that separates like a pregnant pause.

'Uh.'

Andy's in town. He's here to launch his new film *Heat*, reviled by one reviewer as *'a faggoty rehash of* Sunset Boulevard*'*, sticking around after its West Coast premiere to watch David sing 'Andy Warhol' on stage in Santa Monica. Between the song and his spoken introduction he says Andy's name a dozen times. Thousands applaud. Andy goes to the after-party but doesn't linger and leaves early; when asked later, he says David never paid him enough attention.

The Santa Monica shows provide enough of an illusion of success to convince the LA press David is *'a major star'* and the best thing to hit the city *'since Elton'*. Two nights later, Elton hits back. He plays to twelve times as many people who watch him clunk on stage in platform boots and a shiny Uncle Sam suit, a framed picture of Doris Day on the lid of his piano, at intervals joined by a bearded tap-dancing freak wearing a crash helmet, a leotard and a wedding gown attended by two midgets dressed as sailors, a Busby Berkeley chorus line of blonde dancing girls and showers of glitter exploding at the climax of 'Singin' In The Rain'. He gets over a dozen standing ovations. The critics gasp *'flawless'* and *'phenomenal'* then faint for want of adjectives.

After the show, Elton and his manager John retire to their bungalow in the Beverly Hills Hotel. What they do behind its door is still illegal in 46 states. Next door in number 5, David upholds the constitution with Cyrinda.

HIS FLIGHT LANDS in Heathrow early on a grey Sunday morning. Elton steps off wearing silver platforms, loose satin trousers the colour of a bar of Dairy Milk, one of his own tour T-shirts and a rusty fur coat the same shade as David's hair. He makes his way to the customs desk in Terminal 3 where he can see the arrivals hall through the glass partition. Staring back at him are several hundred teenage faces. Many of them black. Some of them start pointing and grinning and banging on the glass. Others mouth his name clear enough for him to read. 'EL-TON!' In that T-shirt under that coat with those trousers and those shoes, wearing those glasses, he can't pretend to be anyone else.

The customs man hands back his passport and waves him through. He walks towards the glass. A sprinkling of blue helmets and peaked caps offers some reassurance. He braces himself. So do the kids. As he steps through the door they suddenly pour towards him, giggling in threes and fours. The police spread apart to intercept them as he turns and runs as best as four-inch platforms allow. He totters out of the terminal straight to the safety of the limousine he knows is waiting outside. He falls in, slamming the door behind him. He looks at his watch. It's 7.30 a.m. He sinks down on the leather and laughs.

What the bloody hell were that lot doing at this godforsaken hour of the Sabbath waiting for *him*?

They weren't. Elton was never their quarry, just an unexpected appetiser. A recognisable pop star in the right place at the wrong time. If he'd stopped to look, he might have noticed the different badges on their pinafores. Some say 'J5'. Others have heart-framed photographs of a toothy teenage boy. Two sets of fans for two sets of brothers, both arriving this morning from America, both responsible for turning Heathrow into the shrieking siege tomorrow's papers make sound like a zombie horror film.

'THE DAY OF THE WEENYBOPPERS'

The first lot arrive moments after Elton's limo speeds into the mist. The weenyboppers were expecting five but in the event they get six of them: Jackie, aged 21; Tito, just turned 19; Jermaine, 17; Marlon, 15; the star, Michael, only 14; and the unexpected baby, little Randy, whose 11th birthday it is today. All smiling, all dressed smartly in fur and leather coats fully prepared for the English winter. Less so the lovely girls of Lambeth climbing up the windows of customs and baggage reclaim.

The thin blue line thickens. The Jacksons emerge. The bobbies circle. The girls charge pell-mell, screaming and tripping, throwing scarves and shoes, hands madly pecking at afros through the scrum of helmets, tumbling out through the doors, shoving, punching and wailing till the quick cruel rev of the exhaust whisks their black princes away. Then sink, spent, to the pavement and wail louder.

The puffing bobbies straighten their clothes and limp back inside the terminal where the remaining girls seem to have multiplied.

That was only round one.

Round two takes place on the roof of Terminal 2, where the weepy young hystericals have been herded in numbers not seen since David Cassidy was here, all eyes on the ground where two Rolls-Royce Phantoms surrounded by police and press await the approaching TWA shuttle bus. Out clamber five perfect specimens of fibrous hair and radioactive teeth, and a small chubby sixth: Alan, 23; Wayne, 22; Merrill, 19; Jay, 17; the star, Donny, only 14; and Little Jimmy, aged 9. The united screech from the kids on the roof is like the slow creaking open of the Gates of Hell. Safe below on God's tarmac, the Osmonds smile up and wave. Above them, girls not much older than Little Jimmy look ready to leap off and impale themselves on either of the two Rolls's Spirits of Ecstasy. The brothers keep waving long enough to satisfy the delirium of those who woke at 2 a.m. to travel several hundred miles to be here. Then, duty done, the motorcade speeds off to the sanctuary of their five-star hotel. The Churchill, just off Oxford Street on Portman Square, not two streets away from Marc's new flat.

The same hotel the Jacksons checked into three hours ago.

Around a thousand kids are already chanting their names outside as their limos pull up. Some of them have cake tins. 'For Donny.' Others wave magazine pictures of Michael. The curtain of night doesn't send them home as the news leaks that the Jacksons are on the seventh floor, the Osmonds the fifth. Heads tilt up in both directions. They yell. They cry. They wait.

They're still there the next day, trying to bribe the other hotel guests to smuggle them in – *'Pleeeease! I've got £1.50!'* – chasing the cars that take the Jacksons off to the London Palladium to join Elton, Liberace, Danny La Rue and Alf Garnett for the Royal Variety Performance in the presence of the Queen Mum. The Jacksons, the only non-white act on the bill, sing a medley of hits. Alf cracks a joke ending 'worse than a family of Pakis next door to you'. In the royal box, We are very amused.

On Tuesday, as Elton and his silver platforms dash back to the States to resume their tour, a crush of Osmonds fans smashes one of the Churchill's plate-glass windows. Not to be outdone, the Jacksons posse cause £5,000 worth of damage to the brothers' limousine outside the Talk of the Town.

Wednesday brings more chaos as the Osmonds resort to decoy Daimlers before heading to *Top of the Pops* to play their new single 'Crazy Horses'. Back at the Churchill, the Jacksons try to ease tensions by giving a free performance on the roof to placate the fans blockading the street below. It sends the blockade ballistic. The police end up dragging eight girls away into custody. Some of them have knives and hammers. None are older than 13.

By Friday, with the Jacksons quietly slipping off to fly to Amsterdam, fears of a riot force Swan & Edgar's department store in Piccadilly Circus to cancel the Osmonds' scheduled visit. It's all too much for Merrill, who by Saturday morning is so feverish he misses his chance to witness yet more girls clinging for life onto limo bonnets when his brothers dash in and out of Broadcasting House for Stewpot's *Junior Choice*. He later recovers, to the relief of the pigtailed maniacs with tickets for that night's sold-out show at the Rainbow, where Donny, in a white rhinestone Elvis suit, sings 'Puppy Love' on the same stage where David sang 'Queen Bitch' eleven weeks ago.

Five miles across town, five very different specimens of American hair and teeth are flapping their chiffon in the faces of a startled crowd of Status Quo fans in Imperial College. As support slots go, it's one of the better crowds the New York Dolls have had since they arrived two weeks ago, buoyed by that *Maker* feature and now gambling on landing a record deal in England. That's why Jagger's here. On the strength of what he'd read in the press he'd been thinking of signing them to the Stones' own label. Until he sees them, when he thinks again. He has fellow Stone Mick Taylor with him for a second opinion. Taylor agrees. 'The worst high school band I ever saw.'

The Dolls still have another week of gigs to fulfil supporting Roxy Music, but in their poky hotel in South Kensington tempers are fraying. It's been downhill ever since last week when they drove the near 200 miles to Liverpool to support Lou Reed. This came as news to Lou, who promptly booted them off his tour before they'd even had a chance to untwist their lipsticks. Johansen is even more uptight because he keeps ringing long distance to New York to speak to Cyrinda, who doesn't seem to be home. Frustrations fester and rows ricochet. Until Billy Doll has enough and disappears to a party in a nearby block of flats opposite the Natural History Museum. Drunk on wine and doped on Quaaludes, he collapses. The other party guests lay him in an empty bathtub, forcing coffee down his throat before leaving him to sober up. Billy is 3,000 miles from home, alone and unconscious in a nonsensical land where children bop to 'Mouldy Old Dough'. What a time, what a place, to choke to death on your own vomit.

Happy new dreams end. Sadder old ones begin.

Not two miles from the cold body of Billy Murcia, a lonely-faced man, all the lonelier-looking for having to wear glasses, sits on a chaise longue in his Marylebone flat, eyes hovering on the book in his hand, ears alert for the postman's ring.

It's now a fortnight since he placed the ad in the *Maker* classifieds. No joy yet, but perhaps today? Just give it time. In a few days he'll be 50, and if five decades have taught him one thing, it's patience. Because it's got to happen. Happen sometime. And maybe this time . . . he'll stay?

NINETEEN

THE BROKEN DOLLS come home to an election landslide for Nixon and the number 1 sound of Johnny Nash. A bright, bright sunshiny day for America. Bright as the razorblade David uses to remove his eyebrows in a hotel chalet in Arizona. His face, smooth as a polished diamond. He does it because he's drunk, because he's unhappy, because after six weeks in America he's going seriously fucking mad. So has everyone else: Nixon's just won with the largest voter turnout and second largest majority in the nation's history.

Nothing's been right for David since he left Los Angeles. Two disastrous nights in San Francisco, the city of the beats. Dead ones in the case of the cattle shed called Winterland, one third full. Another half-empty shambles in Seattle. Then a total flop in Phoenix. That's when the eyebrows come off. The next pencilled dates in Texas are cancelled outright fearing a defeat worse than the Alamo.

Aside from full houses, his marbles and the hairs on his brow, he's also lost the solace of Cyrinda, gone back to New York to face the music of her bereaved Doll boyfriend. Their romance burned out in San Francisco after lost hours wandering its streets of thrift shops, muted-post-horn graffiti and skid row hotels. A promo film for 'The Jean Genie' becomes their rock'n'roll keepsake, David playing sleaze blue Jimmy Dean to Cyrinda's trash orange Marilyn. Their last night together he stood over her naked as she lay in his hotel bath wearing pearls and a long blonde wig. He came and the next morning she went.

'Are you man enough for David Bowie?'

Asks the cover of *Rolling Stone* magazine as the tour plods on through the South, its tired company in need of reinforcements. Cherry steps in to tag with Leee as Defries's advance team when Dai returns to London, physically shattered and emotionally scandalised. David and the Spiders' stagewear is slowly falling to bits. As is RCA's patience with Defries, who's convinced them to keep the tour afloat even as its hull keeps springing new leaks. He has the justification of more 'product' to push now they've reissued two of David's old albums in vamped-up Ziggified picture sleeves. The hope is by the end of the month he should have three LPs in the American Top 200. And he will. Mainly the bottom half. America is only man enough for the English whinnies of Cat Stevens and Rod Stewart, both in its Top 10, and Marc. The US critics wiped their shoes on T. Rex but *The Slider* peaks at 17. David has them shining his but *Ziggy* can't break their Top 80.

As he runs out of time, 'Time' runs out of him in New Orleans where he hears the news about Billy Doll. A song about the dreams that begin and the death that ends and the pointless wanking between. Because when he looks at the albino-pale eyebrowless face staring back at him in the mirror, like a sad clown in a carroty wig, that's all life amounts to. The adolescent wish that brought him here. The constant fear of the plane falling out of the sky. The dismal spunk on the bathroom floor.

Tick-tock, tick-tock.

Watches reset from Pacific to Central to Eastern. Beaten by the South, the tour sensibly retreats back up to Cleveland where it started nine weeks ago in victory, hoping for another. The same venue but this time the bigger of its auditoriums. Two nights, sold out, to three times the crowd, many of them glitterbombed head to toe in homemade 'ZIGGY' T-shirts.

'DON'T THEY ALL LOOK FAAABULOUS?'

She's back.

Angie hasn't been idle. Since Defries banished her to London she's been making herself useful as nursemaid to the remaining Stooges who'd been left behind, bored, broke and Iggyless in a Chelsea mews. Feeling sorry for them, she decided she'd fly them all back home to Ann Arbor in Michigan – at Mainman's expense, without Defries's consent. Once there, she hung around long enough to meet one of their friends, a gorgeous singer named Scott. She thought it might be nice if she brought him along to Cleveland too. To show him to her husband.

On stage at the Public Hall, David wears a pair of Cyrinda's earrings. His left wrist, once adorned with the silver Peruvian bangles first placed there by Angie at his wedding ceremony two and a half years ago, is now naked: a few nights back a fan swiped them off his arm as he reached into the front rows for his customary *'gimme your hands'* finale.

Tonight, Angie, with Scott, watches David unveil another of his new songs, one that came to him in a train observation car somewhere between the lush forests of Oregon and the dead Mojave Desert, called 'Drive-In Saturday'. He tells the crowd it's 'about a future where people have forgotten how to make love'.

Back at the hotel, there's an after-party in David's suite; Angie, of course, is there. When it's over he goes to his room and she to hers. Neither are alone. Nothing is forgotten.

HE LOOKS THIN. Thinner than the last time Ian from Mott saw him three months ago. The kind of thin that shows most in the face, bones poking through skin like a plastic bag filled with broken glass, all the sharper for the hairless brow smooth as a boiled onion. The visage of a man who last week a Louisiana rag called a *'trans-human ambisexual spaceman'*, a description it fits to a Venusian T. The thin head pokes out of a loose Japanese top with matching flared bottoms. On his feet are wooden wedges with thick heels decorated with palm trees. He sits forward on a plump-cushioned camelback sofa, a cigarette between his lips, a reel tape recorder beside him with sprawling leads connected to the stereo in the corner. On the floor, unplugged, a Moog synthesizer. Surrounding him, service trolleys of empty wine bottles, plates, cloches and crumpled white napkins. Outside, the sleepless drone of waitresses yelling checks for hot pastrami, tired sirens and psychotic bums. New York City, 2 a.m.

They can't hear the city for the music. David's spent the last couple of days here recording after his tour ended last week. He's heard Ian is in town on a break in Mott's own shorter American tour so called him over to his 18th-floor suite in the Warwick to play him the new tracks he's been working on. One in particular, his future sex song 'Drive-In Saturday', now arranged by Mick into a heavy interstellar doo-wop. David thinks it's maybe the best thing he's written since 'All The Young Dudes'. That's why he really wants Ian to hear it – so Mott will record it and give him another hit.

Ian listens, chin bobbing to the beat, digging the harmonies, the Philly soul saxes, David's voice and its weird lyrics about people in domes, skin flicks, Mick Jagger and Twiggy. He tries to imagine himself singing it. He can't. The truth is he doesn't want to sing any more of David's songs. 'Dudes' was amazing but 'Dudes' was enough, and Mott still haven't been able to get that one right live. Every time they play it on this tour, it sounds a mess; only David can hit those chorus high notes, which is why Ian has to bark his way through it instead. Apart from anything else, he doesn't think 'Drive-In Saturday' is *that* good a song.

'ISN'T IT GREAT?'

She's still here.

Angie curls on a nearby chair in a silver oriental-style dress. Of course she's still here. The tour is over, the gear loaded away, the groupies all back in school playing catch-up on their times tables. Just him and the wife again, Mr and Mrs Jones. Whatever that means to either of them anymore.

Something. It must. Why else would David have spent the last couple of days re-recording 'The Prettiest Star', the song he wrote for Angie when he asked her to marry him over two years ago? If that isn't still love, even if a guilty, grieving love severely damaged by too many weeks in cocksucking transit, what else is it?

He plays it for Ian as its muse quietly twitches her feet to its rhythm, smiling like a stroked cat. Ian tells him he likes the saxophones. A smile slices David's face like a paper cut. 'I want to add a horn section to the Spiders,' he says, 'three altos and a baritone. Like in Little Richard's band, and all in white suits with wide lapels. And frizzy Mafia hairdos with glitter stuck on.'

The tape reel ends with a strange half-finished instrumental. 'I think it's going to be the title track of the new album,' he tells Ian. 'I'm still working on the words.' Even without them it sounds distinctly David.

The sad funky melody of a trans-human ambisexual spaceman. With palm trees on his feet and no eyebrows.

'It's called "Aladdin Sane" . . .'

'**I MAY EVEN BE MAD ALREADY.**' His mouth says it. His puffy eyes know it. 'I don't know the difference anymore. There is no reality for me.' Marc raises the glass to his lips and sips one of the few realities he can rely on. Alcohol. That and magic powders, and the girls who hover outside his offices in Doughty Street as they used to outside his old flat, and the gold disc inside to remind every reporter who comes in that 'Get It On' sold a million in America, which only proves the stories about him bombing in the States are a vicious lie. 'We sold out Los Angeles in an hour!' And there's *The Slider*, which got to number 17 over there. 'But where are David Bowie and Slade? Not in the Top 100!'

Every interview now, the same comparative questions about the Osmonds, the Jackson 5, Slade and David Bowie. 'There's this position of everyone trying to dethrone Bolan,' he tells them, 'but in fact there's no throne to have and the so-called "top" is a fantasy lost world.' But still they come, and still they ask, and still they chip away at his sanity, one headline at a time.

'When I read things about me, I wonder who they are talking about. Yesterday, I burst out crying for no reason at all. I often get brought down. Many times I've been sitting in a room full of people and I've just wanted to break everything and smash all the windows and scream my head off. I get so mad and so over the edge that I can't snap. I'm like a willow tree.'

The reporter nods awkwardly, wondering when best to change the topic to the threat of David Cassidy. Marc drops another cube of ice in his glass with a sniff. Neither he nor his face on the posters on the walls are smiling.

THE FACE ON THE POSTERS of the walls of Studio C is David's. He's also on the ones hanging below the table with two boom microphones, four glasses of water and four empty chairs which should have been filled 15 minutes ago. The few dozen journalists who've pecked their way through the cheese buffet and made the most of the stony-faced tuxedoed waiters distributing free cider sit patiently, stifling burps, their tape recorders and notebooks ready. A collective buzz as shapes suddenly move through the glass in the control room. The door opens. In walks David, hair like a fox fur muffler, silver earrings, waxwork skin and one of Freddie's suits with triangular shoulder pads chequered turquoise and black. He's followed by Mick, Woody and Trevor, then Defries, cigar wedged between a week's worth of beard, in a leather coat. David and the Spiders take their seats. He leans in to the microphone and introduces them one by one, right to left.

'And I *am* David Bowie,' he adds.

The press conference is intended as his gracious end-of-tour farewell. David is supposed to talk about what a success it's been, how it's stimulated the songs he's been writing for his next album, and his plans to return here next February. The reporters would rather talk about the rumours they've heard about the tour losing money: that RCA have had to underwrite it by many hundreds of thousands of dollars, that attendances were poor and that the William Morris Agency are suing David for breach of contract.

Over in the corner, Defries quietly chokes on his cigar.

David blinks, smiling feebly. 'I can't comment,' he says.

What hair colouring does he use?

'A German brand. I can't pronounce it.'

Why does he write gay songs?

'Who doesn't like gay people?'

What's the first song he ever listened to?

'"Purple People Eater".'

What's been his favourite thing about America?

'The people.'

And now that it's over, what are his lasting impressions?

'The biggest thing that hit me about America – and I'm not saying it doesn't apply to England as well – is I feel the American is the loneliest person in the world. There's a general feeling of a lack of security and a need for warmth in people that's so sad. So many people are not aware of being in America . . . You get on a train and it keeps going. America just goes on and on and you think – will it ever end?'

He pauses, thinking of the right full stop.

'I think the whole country has the aura of being built and conditioned by McDonald's and Woolworths.'

IN THE CAPITAL of the United States of McDonald's and Woolworths, in the East Wing of the White House, the newly re-elected president by a landslide, Richard Milhous Nixon, his wife Pat, his youngest daughter Julie, his close friend 'Bebe', and the wife of one of his loyal campaigners, Helene, retire to the president's private movie theatre after a most pleasant dinner together. Tonight's chosen entertainment is a brand-new film, so new that Nixon is watching it the same night as its world premiere in Times Square: the president has that power. Nixon loves watching movies almost as much as he loves wiretapping his political opposition and dropping bombs on civilians in Southeast Asia. Two nights after he won the election he celebrated by watching *The Great Escape*. He should enjoy this film too because its poster says it's 'ONE OF THE GREATEST ESCAPE ADVENTURES EVER!' The White House projector starts rolling at two minutes past 9 p.m. when the Nixons and their friends settle down to the story of a luxury cruise liner setting out from New York in December, bound for Europe, capsized by a freak tsunami that drowns most of the crew and passengers save a few plucky survivors.

The day after the president watches *The Poseidon Adventure*, in a cold December in New York, David boards the Royal Hellenic Mail Ship *Ellinis*, bound for England. It will take him seven days. A flight would take him seven hours. He still thinks it's safer.

TWENTY

STILL SAFER THAN A TIN CAN far above the world. As the *Ellinis* weighs anchor and heads slowly out into the Atlantic, the last two men who will ever stand on the surface of the moon are spending their final day collecting samples of rock. Yesterday, they stuck the national flag of the United States of McDonald's and Woolworths in the lunar crust and saluted it, just as their president sat down to watch a disaster movie roughly a quarter of a million miles away on the distant blue marble they call home. Tomorrow, they'll be woken up by Houston playing them Strauss's *Also Sprach Zarathustra* from *2001: A Space Odyssey* a few minutes before their lunar module blasts off from the surface to dock safely with their third pilot in the *Apollo 17* command vessel. Once they jettison everything they don't need, they'll return to Earth in a blunt cone-shaped spaceship weighing a little more than two Rolls-Royces, serenaded by more music from the Doors, Roberta Flack and the Carpenters. Nobody at NASA is dumb enough to play them 'Space Oddity'. Even if they did, the crew of *Apollo 17* wouldn't know what it was.

This is why 'Space Oddity' is the last song David performs in America before he steps onto the gangplank. RCA want to release it as a single in the States, where it was never successful first time around, and need a promo film to accompany it. With the little energy left in his thinning bones he sits in their studio and mimes along to a depressing song he wrote and recorded over three years ago, back when his hair wasn't red and he still had eyebrows on his face. He looks tired and sad and lonely, and slightly crazy. Like an astronaut who knows he will never see home again.

But he will. One week and an ocean away, the United Kingdom of Wimpy and Woolworths waits to re-embrace him with adverts for back rub and coupons for tuppence off Bird's Eye cod in sauce. In titpacked tabloids, every gang rape in the country is still being blamed on *A Clockwork Orange* and *A Clockwork Orange* is still only being shown exclusively in one cinema in London's Leicester Square. In horn-rims, Mary Whitehouse keeps fighting filth in all its satanic forms, even if she appears to be the only Christian in England who seriously believes Chuck Berry's 'My Ding-A-Ling' should be banned for promoting 'mass child molestation'. In Kensington, the Mr Freedom boutique has closed and with it the lid of glam's premature coffin. On TV, the nation's favourite show *Till Death Us Do Part* has just filmed its Christmas special with a bar-propping cameo from David's friend Dana. On the newsstands, the *Maker* is now neck and neck in the sales race with their old rivals the *NME*, who snootily dismiss Lou's *Transformer* as *'incredibly irritating'* and blow raspberries at the experimental German band Kraftwerk for being *'a numbing bore'*. In *Jackie*, between posters of David Cassidy and Gary Glitter, Elton names *Ziggy Stardust* his favourite album of the year, adding, 'I just hope David doesn't go too far or freaky.' In *Gay News*, David is hailed 'Artist of the Year' while 'Group of the Year' goes to Roxy Music. In Roxy Music, Andy Mackay decides 'Bolan is much better than Bowie' because David 'wants to be too serious' whereas Marc 'just wants to be a straightforward rock star'. In the never straightforward Top 10, Marc's scintillating new song about picking foxes off trees, 'Solid Gold Easy Action', can't get to number 1 for Little Jimmy Osmond's 'Long Haired Lover From Liverpool'. Nor can Jimmy's big brothers with a song about horses, nor Slade with a song about a San Francisco hippie chick, nor Michael Jackson with a song about a rat, nor Elton with a song about a crocodile, nor John and Yoko with a song about Christmas. Nor David with 'The Jean Genie'. But he's getting closer every day. Just like his ship to the shores of Southampton.

In his spacious stateroom, David flicks open a book to try and ignore the tremendous sense of foreboding that's plagued him since before he set sail. A premonition of imminent catastrophe, like a century dying fast, or a third world war, or an iceberg straight ahead. A 'Five Years' feeling like wearing goggles tinted the colour of the end of the world. He can't blame it all on the emotional shrapnel of three months touring America. He was like this before. He's always been like it. He said so, months ago, back in England when he'd only just started being Ziggy, how he always worried about dying, in the sky, on the road, or even at sea, or even being killed on stage, because sooner or later, he just knew, that one day a big artiste was going to die dramatically in concert. 'And I keep thinking,' he'd said, 'it's bound to be me.'

The ship's course is steady. He turns to the first page.

'It was clearly going to be a bad crossing . . .'

He looks up, helping himself to another cigarette. Across the cabin, Angie is powdering her face in the mirror. He stares at the back of her head long enough for her eyes to catch his. In her mirror . . . *his mirror . . . his spotlight, his battery, his shield, his darer of dreams and his spine when he has none* . . . they look at one another, saying nothing. Neither has to. She keeps on dabbing. He clicks his lighter. They both look away again. His eyes drop back to his book.

'Already there was a vague depression gathering at the top of his head . . .'

David continues reading the 40-year-old tale of a debauched jazz-age England between the wars, not so old he doesn't identify with its antiquity. Haddon Hall wafts from its pages in homesick reveries of Greta Garbo, Lalique glass and men who drive Rileys. His home. His friends.

'Oh, Bright Young People!'

His son.

Christ! How many light years is three months in the quickgrow mind of a toddler? What words has Zowie learned since he last held him? How much bigger has he grown? Will he still recognise him? Even without eyebrows?

'I'm not a very good father.'

He'd said that to a journalist back in the summer.

'Zowie's a lovely companion and fabulous as a person but I'm very irresponsible. Angie's far more responsible than I am.'

Yes. He'd said that too.

He closes the book and lays it down on the table by the ashtray, face up.

Vile Bodies.

Words for unfinished songs begin to scour the inside of his skull. The foreboding, again. He reaches for a pen and paper.

Through his cabin window the low winter sun has already set. Soon he will dress for dinner and he and Angie will step out, arm in arm, to a boat rocking with Australian accents, all gawping and gasping at the sensational Mr and Mrs Jones sat in the Waikiki Room as conspicuous as a couple of giant parakeets. And perhaps afterwards a drink and a soft seat in the Outrigger Bar, or a quick bracing step out on deck. Because at night, looking out over the ocean, it really could be any time. 1972. 1939. 1914. The end of a century or the start of it. There is just the blackness of the sea below and the infinity of the universe above. And somewhere within it three men in a tin can racing home between the stars, who David wouldn't see even if he knew they were there.

BOWIE**DISCOGRAPHY**72

January   **'Changes'**
b/w 'Andy Warhol'
RCA Victor 2160.

April   **'Starman'**
b/w 'Suffragette City'
RCA Victor 2199. Reached number 10 in the UK charts in the last week of July.

June   ***The Rise And Fall Of Ziggy Stardust And The Spiders From Mars***
'Five Years', 'Soul Love', 'Moonage Daydream', 'Starman', 'It Ain't Easy' / 'Lady Stardust', 'Star', 'Hang On To Yourself', 'Ziggy Stardust', 'Suffragette City', 'Rock 'N' Roll Suicide'
RCA Victor SF 8287. David's first album to make the UK Top 10, climbing to number 6 in September, its highest chart placing of 1972; it later peaked at number 5 in February 1973.

VARIOUS ARTISTS
Glastonbury Fayre
'Supermen'
Revelation REV 1/2/3. Triple album compilation to raise funds against losses incurred by the organisers of the 1971 Glastonbury Festival. David's contribution is the Spiders' re-recording of a track from The Man Who Sold The World *(as listed without the definite article).*

July   **MOTT THE HOOPLE**
'All The Young Dudes'
b/w 'One Of The Boys'
CBS S8217. A-side written, co-arranged and produced by David,
who also plays saxophone and sings backing vocals. Reached number 3
in the UK charts in the first week of September.

September **'John, I'm Only Dancing'**
b/w 'Hang On To Yourself'
RCA Victor 2263. The first single listed as 'a Mainman Production'.
Reached number 12 in the second week of October.

    MOTT THE HOOPLE
All The Young Dudes
'Sweet Jane', 'Momma's Little Jewel', 'All The Young Dudes',
'Sucker', 'Jerkin' Crocus' / 'One Of The Boys', 'Soft Ground',
'Ready For Love – After Lights', 'Sea Diver'
CBS S65184. Produced and co-arranged by David, who also wrote,
plays saxophone and sings backing on the title track. Peaked at 21 in
the UK album charts in September.

November **LOU REED**
Transformer
'Vicious', 'Andy's Chest', 'Perfect Day', 'Hangin' Round', 'Walk
On The Wild Side' / 'Make Up', 'Satellite Of Love', 'Wagon
Wheel', 'New York Telephone Conversation', 'I'm So Free',
'Goodnight Ladies'
RCA Victor LSP-4807. Produced by David and Mick Ronson, who
both co-arranged with Lou. The album didn't chart in '72 but reached
number 13 in September 1973.

    Space Oddity
'Space Oddity', 'Unwashed And Somewhat Slightly Dazed',
'Letter To Hermione', 'Cygnet Committee' / 'Janine', 'An
Occasional Dream', 'The Wild Eyed Boy From Freecloud',
'God Knows I'm Good', 'Memory Of A Free Festival'

RCA Victor LSP-4813. Retitled repackage of David's eponymous second album from 1969 in a new Ziggy portrait sleeve; initial copies came with a free colour poster. Released simultaneously with the similarly revamped The Man Who Sold The World *(see below). Both also carried new sleeve notes establishing David as 'a Mainman artist'. This version of the album reached number 17 in August 1973.*

The Man Who Sold The World
'The Width Of A Circle', 'All The Madmen', 'Black Country Rock', 'After All' / 'Running Gun Blues', 'Saviour Machine', 'She Shook Me Cold', 'The Man Who Sold The World', 'The Supermen'
RCA Victor LSP-4816. Repackage of David's third album recorded in 1970 in a new Ziggy portrait sleeve; initial copies came with a free black-and-white poster. This version reached number 23 in September 1973.

'The Jean Genie'
b/w 'Ziggy Stardust'
RCA Victor 2302. Ended the year at number 16 on the way to its UK chart peak of number 2 in January 1973.

LOU REED
'Walk On The Wild Side'
b/w 'Perfect Day'
RCA Victor 2303. Produced by David and Mick Ronson. Seven months later it reached number 10 in June 1973.

BOWIE**SOURCES**72

AUTHOR **INTERVIEWS** for the *Bowie Odyssey* series in person, by telephone and email correspondence with Dai Davies, Wendy Kirby, Robin Mayhew, Laurence Myers, Kris Needs, Mark Pritchett, Michael Watts, Barrie Wentzell and Anya Wilson. Additional information from this author's past interviews with David Johansen, Arthur Kane and Sylvain Sylvain of the New York Dolls (2004) and Iggy Pop (2010). Very special thanks to Tom Doyle who interviewed Tony Defries in 2021 for *Mojo* magazine and kindly shared his transcript with this author.

The memoirs of Angie Bowie, *Free Spirit* (Mushroom Books, 1981) and *Backstage Passes: Life on the Wild Side with David Bowie* (with Patrick Carr, Putnam, 1993); David Bowie's own words as included in Mick Rock's photography collection *Moonage Daydream: The Life and Times of Ziggy Stardust* (Universe, 2005); Cyrinda Foxe-Tyler, *Dream On: Livin' on the Edge with Steven Tyler and Aerosmith* (Signet, 1997); Ian Hunter, *Diary of a Rock'n'Roll Star* (Panther, 1974); Elton John, *Me* (Macmillan, 2019); Bettye Kronstad, *Perfect Day: An Intimate Portrait of Life with Lou Reed* (Jawbone Press, 2016); Robin Mayhew, *Ambition* (self-published, 2016); Laurence Myers, *Hunky Dory (Who Knew?)* (B&B Books, 2019); Kris Needs, *Needs Must: A Very Rock'n'Roll Story* (Virgin, 1999); Lisa Robinson, *There Goes Gravity: A Life in Rock'n'Roll* (Riverhead Books, 2014); Sylvain Sylvain (with Dave Thompson), *There's No Bones in Ice Cream: Sylvain Sylvain's Story of the New York Dolls* (Omnibus Press, 2018); Cherry Vanilla, *Lick Me: How I Became Cherry Vanilla* (Chicago Review Press, 2010); Woody

Woodmansey, *Spider from Mars: My Life with Bowie* (Sidgwick & Jackson, 2016); and Tony Zanetta, as detailed in his and Henry Edwards' *Stardust: The David Bowie Story* (McGraw-Hill, 1986). Also the recollections of Suzi Ronson as included in *The Moth: All These Wonders: 49 New True Stories*, edited by Catherine Burn (Serpent's Tail, 2017).

The chronology of Bowie historian Kevin Cann's *Any Day Now: David Bowie: The London Years 1947–1974* (Adelita, 2010).

Chapter Two is indebted to *A Clockwork Orange* by Anthony Burgess, first published in 1962; glossaries of Burgess's Nadsat language as used in that chapter are available in all contemporary editions of the novel, and online.

Other works: Joe Ambrose, *Gimme Danger: The Story of Iggy Pop* (Omnibus Press, 2004); Nina Antonia, *The New York Dolls: Too Much Too Soon* (Omnibus Press, 2005); Victoria Broackes and Geoffrey Marsh, *David Bowie Is* (V&A Publications, 2013); Neil Cossar, *David Bowie: I Was There* (Red Planet, 2017); Anthony DeCurtis, *Lou Reed: A Life* (John Murray, 2017); Tom Doyle, *Captain Fantastic: Elton John's Stellar Trip Through the '70s* (Polygon, 2017); Henry Fisher, *Report of an Inquiry by the Hon. Sir Henry Fisher into the Circumstances Leading to the Trial of Three Persons on Charges Arising Out of the Death of Maxwell Confait and the Fire at 27 Doggett Road, London SE6* (Her Majesty's Stationery Office, 1977); Peter and Leni Gillman, *Alias David Bowie* (New English Library, 1987); Gary Glitter (with Lloyd Bradley), *Leader: The Autobiography* (Ebury Press, 1991); Peter Guralnick and Ernst Jorgensten, *Elvis: Day by Day* (Ballantine Books, 1999); Jerry Hopkins, *Bowie* (Macmillan, 1985) and *Elvis* (Simon & Schuster, 1971); Dylan Jones, *David Bowie: A Life* (Preface, 2017); Lesley-Ann Jones, *Hero: David Bowie* (Hodder & Stoughton, 2016) and *Ride a White Swan: The Lives and Death of Marc Bolan* (Hodder & Stoughton, 2012); Wendy Leigh, *Bowie: The Biography* (Gallery Books, 2014); Jill Liddington (ed.), *Time Out's Book of London* (Time Out, 1972); Cliff McLenehan, *Marc Bolan: 1947–1977 A Chronology* (Helter Skelter, 2002); William H. Miller, *The Chandris Liners* (Carmania Press, 1993); Paul Morley, *The Age of Bowie* (Simon & Schuster, 2016); Vincent Mulchrone, *Queen Elizabeth 2* (Pitkin Pictorials, 1969); Kris Needs, *The Thin White Book: A History of David Bowie and Friars Aylesbury* (Friars Aylesbury, 2017); Chris O'Leary, *Rebel Rebel: All the Songs of David Bowie from '64 to '76* (Zero Books, 2015); Mark Paytress, *Bolan: The Rise and Fall of a 20th Century Superstar* (Omnibus Press, 2006); Nicholas Pegg, *The Complete David Bowie* (expanded and updated edition) (Titan Books, 2016); Christopher Sandford, *Bowie: Loving the Alien* (Little, Brown, 1996);

George Tremlett, *The David Bowie Story* (Futura, 1974); Paul Trynka, *Iggy Pop: Open Up and Bleed* (Sphere, 2007) and *Starman: David Bowie: The Definitive Biography* (Little, Brown, 2011); Evelyn Waugh, *Vile Bodies* (Penguin, 1938); Weird and Gilly, *Mick Ronson: The Spider with the Platinum Hair* (Independent Music Press, 2009); Theodore H. White, *The Making of the President 1972* (Scribner, 1973); Ellen Willis, *Out of the Vinyl Deeps: Ellen Willis on Rock Music* (University of Minnesota Press, 2011).

Key period broadcasts and theatrical releases referenced: *A Clockwork Orange* (Hawk Films, 1971), direction and screenplay by Stanley Kubrick, based on the novel by Anthony Burgess; *Cabaret* (Allied Artists, 1972), directed by Bob Fosse, screenplay by Jay Allen; *Love Thy Neighbour*, 'The Housewarming Party' (Thames Television, 1972), written by Vince Powell and Harry Driver; *The Royal Variety Performance* (BBC, 1972), *Till Death Us Do Part* sketch written by Johnny Speight.

Period newspapers and magazines. National: *Daily Express, Daily Mail, Daily Mirror, Daily Telegraph, Guardian, News of the World, Nova, Observer, Radio Times, The Sun, Sunday Mirror, Sunday People, Sunday Times* (and *Magazine*), *TV Times, Vogue*. Regional: *Beckenham Journal, Bromley Times, Evening News* (London), *Evening Standard* (London), *Hull & Yorkshire Times, Lincolnshire Standard, Manchester Evening News, Telegraph & Argus* (Bradford), *South Yorkshire Times, Walsall Observer*.

Pop/rock and teenage: *Beat Instrumental, Bolan* (1972 *Melody Maker* Special), *Cream, Disc and Music Echo* (as *Disc* from April '72), *Fabulous 208, Honey* (as *Honey & Vanity Fair* from May '72), *Jackie, Look-In, Melody Maker, Mirabelle, Music Scene, New Musical Express, 19, Petticoat, Record Mirror, Sounds*; with very special thanks to the archives of Tom Sheehan.

Counterculture/adult/gay and women's lib: *Come Together, Curious, Frendz, Gay News, Ink, International Times, Lunch, Spare Rib, Time Out*.

American publications: *After Dark, Andy Warhol's Interview, Billboard, Cashbox, Cavalier, Circus, Cleveland Press, Creem, Fusion, Life, Los Angeles Times, New York Times, New Yorker, Newsweek, Rolling Stone, Variety, Village Voice*.

For extra help and facilitating, many thanks to Barney Hoskyns of rocksbackpages.com, Louise North at the BBC Written Archives Centre in Reading, Michael Odell, Rachél Ruderman, David Stopps, Aki Sukita and Matt Turner. And with severe gratitude to the staff at the British Library for all their efforts to remain operational in recent trying times.

BOWIEIMAGES72

FRONT COVER
David Bowie *is* Ziggy Stardust (Paperback © Masayoshi Sukita; Hardback special edition © Chris Foster/Shutterstock).

IMAGES page 1
'Nothing is ever going to be the same again.' Already a Starman, not yet a lad insane, New York City, September '72 (© Michael Ochs/Getty Images).

IMAGES pages 2–3
Top row (left to right): Rock and rouge – 'I always had the conception that aliens from other planets could possibly have red hair. If they came, I wanted them not to be freaked.' – David, November '72 (© Mainman/Pennebaker/Kobal/Shutterstock); Young dudes, Belfast, celebrating another IRA killing of a British soldier, April '72 (© Alex Bowie/Getty Images); Young dudes, London, in an anti-school march of mobilised truants, May '72 (© Mirrorpix); Young droog Alex kicks the world into touch in *A Clockwork Orange* (© Everett Collection/Alamy).
Bottom row (left to right): The look of love – Birmingham Bolanites prepare for a night of T. Rextasy, June '72 (© Michael Putland/Getty Images); The look of decadence – the divine Liza Minnelli in *Cabaret* (© Silver Screen Collection/Getty Images); The look of boop-boop-a-doop – Twig the Wonderkid gets '72 fashions flapping in *The Boy Friend*

(© Landmark Media/Alamy); The look of hate – the racist face of anti-immigration England, August '72 (© Keystone Press/Alamy).

IMAGES pages 4–5
The Glammer Twins. Left: David Jones of Brixton, born 1947 (© Masayoshi Sukita). **Right:** Mark Feld of Hackney, born 1947 (© Michael Putland/Getty Images).

IMAGES pages 6–7
Top row (left to right): Pancake factor number one – the New York Dolls in London, 29 October 1972; stood behind the seated David Johansen, left to right, are Billy Murcia, who died one week after this photo was taken, Johnny Thunders, Arthur 'Killer' Kane and Sylvain Sylvain (© P. Felix/Getty Images); Time takes a cigarette – David in his Freddie Burretti Ziggy suit, Haddon Hall, 1972 (© Michael Putland/Getty Images).
Bottom row (left to right): Too much too soon – the dangerously famous David Cassidy (© Globe Photos/Shutterstock); Too much to bear – the Pulitzer Prize-winning photo of naked nine-year-old Phan Thi Kim Phuc escaping a napalm attack in the South Vietnam village of Trảng Bàng on 8 June 1972 (© Nick Ut/AP/Shutterstock); Too much too young – Napalm-free nine-year-old Little Jimmy Osmond was number 1 in Britain over Christmas '72 as his country's president dropped bombs on Vietnamese hospitals (© Anwar Hussein/Getty Images).

IMAGES page 8
Somewhere under the Rainbow, Finsbury Park, August '72 (© Masayoshi Sukita).

ENDPAPERS
Starman in civvies (© Masayoshi Sukita).

Picture research and layout concept by Simon Goddard.

THANKYOU

To the generous assistance of the men from *Melody Maker*,
unquestionably the world's greatest music paper in 1972,
Michael Watts and Barrie Wentzell.

For good wining, dining and deep memory mining,
Mark Pritchett (pizza, Beckenham)
and Dai Davies (fish'n'chips, Tenby).

Kris Needs, timeless child of the revolution.

The droogie Omnibus odyssey squad of David Barraclough,
Imogen Gordon Clark, Fabrice Couillerot, Judith Forshaw, Greg Morton,
David Stock and Debra Geddes at Great Northern PR.

Wham bam to Kevin Pocklington at the North Literary Agency
and a whopping thank you ma'am to my brilliant editor Alison Rae.

Tom Doyle – it's a mug's game.

And to Sylv, who loves Ziggy but not half as much as Iggy.

DAVID BOWIE
will return in

BOWIE**ODYSSEY**73

COMING 2023